THE HIGHFIELDS STORY

*An Experimental Treatment Project
for Youthful Offenders*

Lloyd W. McCorkle
Albert Elias
F. Lovell Bixby

HENRY HOLT AND COMPANY   NEW YORK

BARKLIE McKEE HENRY, FORMER MEMBER OF
THE STATE BOARD OF CONTROL, STATE OF
NEW JERSEY, WHOSE UNFLAGGING SUPPORT
WAS A CONSTANT SOURCE OF INSPIRATION.

Foreword

by Ernest W. Burgess

HIGHFIELDS IS UNIQUE AMONG PROJECTS IN THE TREATMENT OF JU-
venile delinquency.

First of all, it was set up on an experimental basis for five years
to try out the practical value of certain ideas held by Dr. F.
Lovell Bixby, Director, Correction and Parole, Department of
Institutions and Agencies, State of New Jersey, and Lloyd W.
McCorkle, now Warden of the State Prison at Trenton, New
Jersey.

They were vitally interested in finding out if a new type of
treatment center could be introduced—one which had none of
the institutional patterns of a reformatory but which would ex-
emplify the new knowledge of the nature and causes of juvenile
delinquency obtained by psychological and sociological research.

Second, the project was designed to find answers to the following questions.

(1) Could a small residential center, housing twenty boys with
a serious delinquency record under a small staff of four to six persons in charge, be set up and operate successfully?

(2) Could an atmosphere of rehabilitation be established
among the boys that would counteract the existence and growth
of delinquent attitudes and behavior?

(3) Would the boys participate freely and frankly in sessions
of guided group interaction?

(4) Would they be able to make progress in gaining insight
into the factors in their background and experience which had

led them to enter and to continue in a career of delinquency?

(5) Would they at the end of three or four months residence in Highfields have achieved a determination to give up a delinquent for a law-abiding career?

(6) Would they in comparison with a similar group of boys with reformatory experience show as good or even better a record of remaining nondelinquent?

(7) If Highfields was successful would it be because of the personality of its first superintendent or would it be due to ideas and methods that were communicable and therefore could be transmitted to a successor?

The experience of Highfields has now provided answers to these questions.

(1) *The Feasibility of a Residential Center.* Highfields opened with its first group of boys and a staff of four persons. The boys were not committed but came as a condition of probation. There was faith but not certainty that the Center could be operated successfully without guards and without the other precautions against escapes of the large custodial reformatory. There was nothing to prevent all the boys from running away and thus putting an end to a noble experiment.

The idea of permissiveness was carried still further. There was a minimum of regulations. The boys were privileged to spend their free time in informal association. They were told on admission that no effort would be made to prevent their leaving the Center. The one deterrent was their knowledge that an escape was a violation of probation and would result in a new appearance before the juvenile court judge who had sent them to Highfields.

(2) *Creating an Atmosphere of Rehabilitation.* How could an atmosphere of rehabilitation be created? It is generally agreed that in a reformatory, institutional patterns of thinking and acting tend to develop which array the boys against the staff of the institution.

A central problem of a reformatory is the difficulty of establishing an atmosphere favorable to rehabilitation. Yet this is, or should be, the chief objective of a reformatory if it is to live up to its name. Many factors operate against such an atmosphere. First, there is the large size of the institution which focuses attention on the mechanics of administration rather than on interpersonal relations of the residents. Then there are rules and regulations which emphasize regimentation and which have to be enforced.

Also, there is the development of institutionalized patterns of behavior by which the boy seeks to evade or break the rules and regulations.

Finally, as a result of these influences, the group influence operates to maintain and even to intensify delinquent attitudes. Accordingly the reformatory, instead of rehabilitating the boy, tends rather to provide further education in delinquency.

(3) *The Nature of Guided Group Interaction.* Rehabilitation begins with changes in attitudes. But how can these be brought about? The boys entering Highfields have for years identified themselves as delinquents. Their close friends are delinquent. Group pressure has generally pushed and pulled them into delinquency and prevented their rehabilitation. Most delinquents feel rejected and discriminated against by their parents. They generally manifest strong emotional reactions, particularly against their fathers, but often against their mothers, brothers, and sisters. By the time they are confronted with law-enforcing agencies they have developed strong ego defenses. They do not take the responsibility for their delinquency. Instead, they tend to blame others—their parents, their associates, and society.

The whole Highfields experience is directed toward piercing through these strong defenses against rehabilitation, toward undermining delinquent attitudes, and toward developing a self-conception favorable to reformation. The sessions on guided group interaction are especially directed to achieve this objective.

Guided group interaction has the merit of combining the psychological and the sociological approaches to the control of human behavior. The psychological approach aims to change the self-conception of the boy from a delinquent to a nondelinquent. But this process involves changing the mood of the boy from impulses to law breaking to impulses to be law abiding.

To accomplish rehabilitation, the sociological approach is also needed. The insight of sociology is to reverse the process by which the group inducts a boy into delinquency and compels him to continue in it. In guided group interaction, the influence of the group is directed to free the boy from being controlled by delinquent association and to give him the desire and inner strength to be autonomous.

(4) *The Process of Guided Group Interaction.* Guided group interaction is based on psychological and sociological conceptions. But psychological and sociological terms are not used in the sessions.

Only two concepts are voiced by the boys. The first is that of "problem." What is my problem? How did I become a problem to myself and others? How can I go about to solve my problem?

The second concept is that of "progress." Have I made progress in understanding my problem? Am I making progress in solving my problem?

The chapter on Guided Group Interaction presents materials on the ways in which the boys get insight into their behavior, accept responsibility for it, and change their attitudes and conduct. It also shows how the group participates as a unit in the analysis of the behavior of a member and powerfully influences transformations of attitudes.

(5) *Time as a Factor in Rehabilitation.* How long does it take to obtain changes in attitude that may be expected to persist after the boy returns to his community? Highfields has operated on the assumption that three to four months would be adequate. Most reformatories adhere to a minimum residence of twelve months.

The experience of Highfields seems to justify the value of a short period. The boys sent to Highfields are, in general, normal except for their delinquency and antisocial attitudes. Only a few are admitted unintentionally who have deep-seated psychological difficulties.

It can therefore be concluded that the short period of residence in Highfields is adequate for the changing of attitudes of the normal delinquent boy.

(6) *Evaluation of the Success of the Project.* Studies by the Gluecks in Massachusetts and by Shaw and associates in Illinois have revealed the high rate of recidivism of boys after their release from reformatories and industrial schools. It seemed, therefore, desirable to compare the percentage of recidivism of boys with Highfields experience with those who had been released from Annandale, the New Jersey state reformatory. This comparison was pertinent because the boys sent to Highfields would presumably have been committed to Annandale had Highfields not been founded.

Chapter 10 presents a telling account of the much lower percentage of boys with three to four months' Highfields experience who became delinquent after return to the community than of the boys with twelve or more months' residence at Annandale.

The findings are all the more convincing because of the careful control of the factors which might have been responsible for the more favorable outcome of the Highfields boys. The boys in both groups are from Essex County, in which Newark, the largest city in the state, is located. The lower recidivism rates for Highfields as compared with Annandale still hold when the following factors are held constant: number of years of schooling, marital status of parents, residence, race, and age of admission to Highfields or Annandale.

The findings presented in this chapter confirm those found by Dr. Ashley Weeks in his comparative evaluation of the lower recidivism rates for Highfields than for Annandale, reported in a separate volume. Weeks' conclusions, however, were open to the criticism that judges selected cases for Highfields which were more likely to succeed, while sending those more likely to fail to Annandale. This objection was met in the other evaluation by choosing boys from Annandale who were committed there before Highfields opened, but who were of the type that the juvenile court judge would later send to Highfields. The results of the two independent evaluations greatly strengthen the conclusion that Highfields is much more effective in the rehabilitation of delinquents than is the conventional reformatory.

(7) *Change of Superintendents.* At the end of two years' service,

Dr. McCorkle resigned as superintendent of Highfields. Mr. Albert Elias, who had served as intern at Highfields for three months while on leave of absence from the Sheridan reformatory in Illinois, was appointed to succeed him.

The change in superintendents was a clear-cut test of the objection that the success of Highfields might be due to the personality of the first superintendent rather than to the ideas embodied in the project. The continued success of Highfields under the new superintendent demonstrated that the project was not dependent on one personality. The success was due to basic principles and techniques that were communicable and could be learned by other persons.

This book provides all those interested in the problem of delinquency and rehabilitation of delinquents with a description of the philosophy, organization, and operation of Highfields. It presents a vivid picture of the daily life of the boys at work, at leisure, and in the group sessions.

The question is sure to be raised by readers, "Can Highfields be reproduced in our state?"

The provisional answer is that it can under certain conditions. The first is that it have the full and sympathetic support of the agency or department in which it will be operated. The second is that the cases for admission be selected as described for Highfields. The third is that the superintendent be carefully chosen and have or receive experience in guided group interaction, if possible, at Highfields.

A further question is pertinent: "Can Highfields be extended to include other types of boys than those participating in the five-year's demonstration?"

The final answer to this question can only be given after further experimentation. Probably these new demonstrations would lead to a modified form of Highfields designed specifically for the type of boys to be selected for residents.

Preface

WE TAKE THIS OPPORTUNITY TO GRATEFULLY ACKNOWLEDGE OUR INDEBTED-ness to some of the many persons without whose understanding and encouragement Highfields could never have become a reality. Among them was the late Samuel Lewisohn, scholar, statesman, and civic leader, whose vision in penal affairs led him to encourage the New York Foundation, Inc., to make a substantial financial contribution in an untried venture. These funds, augmented by a grant from Mr. and Mrs. Douglas MacNeil, made possible the activation of the Highfields project and paid its major expenses for the first two years of its operation.

Vincent Astor and trustees of the Vincent Astor Foundation, in addition to supporting the research and evaluation of Highfields, made money available for an internship at the project and generously assisted in the publication of this volume.

From Sanford Bates, the former Commissioner, Department of Institutions and Agencies, State of New Jersey, and his successor, John W. Tramburg, and members of the State Board of Control, Highfields received unfailing support and encouragement. New Jersey's Governor Robert B. Meyner and former Governor Alfred E. Driscoll gave strong executive support to this novel idea and made possible its firm and continuing place in the pattern of New Jersey's correctional resources.

Without the cooperation of the New Jersey judiciary and particularly those judges dealing with juvenile offenders, the Highfields idea would have remained a dream. Finally, we are everlastingly indebted to New Jersey's county probation departments and particularly the many probation officers who were strong friends of Highfields in times of trouble and need.

To Professor Jack Reilly of Rutgers University who read the manuscript, we are obligated for many helpful suggestions. Mrs. Allan Cox, secretary at the project, was responsible for enlivening the manuscript with the charts which she prepared.

L.W.Mc.C.
A.E.
F.L.B.

Trenton, New Jersey
October 1, 1957

Table of Contents

I

Introduction to Highfields

WHEN A BOY ARRIVES AT HIGHFIELDS, THE ONLY FORMAL ORIENTA-
tion which he receives involves filling out a small admission card
which is used for identification purposes only and a brief discussion with the director regarding fixed rules. Also, each boy is
invited to ask any questions which he may have regarding Highfields. Then he is introduced to the other personnel and to any
boys who happen to be around the house. Usually, boys arrive
about lunch time and, after eating, they are assigned a bed and
then put to work. By the time the group meetings begin at seven
o'clock in the evening, the new boy has met all the other boys and
has been exposed to a program of informal orientation by the
other boys. It has become customary at Highfields over the years
for new boys to be greeted in a certain way. Usually, word is received by the boys that a new admission is arriving on a particular
day. When the boys return from work in the late afternoon, they
dash into the house and scurry around looking for the new boy.
Once they have located him, they begin throwing questions at
him from all sides. Sometimes he may have a friend here or he
may have heard of one or two boys who are at the project. This
makes his introduction to the peer-group life much easier. However, by this time every boy in the house has developed a conception of the new boy as well as a picture of how he is going to
relate with him, however vague that image may be. Needless to
say, these images will change as time goes by.

A more complete picture of how a boy meets the Highfields
social world is presented in the following description of what
happened to one boy during his first day of residence.

Roy arrived at Highfields, accompanied by his probation officer, at about noon. The director, the probation officer, and Roy had lunch together. During this period, of almost a half hour, the probation officer and the director conversed with each other, while Roy kept a respectful silence. Once the probation officer urged Roy to eat more food, which he did. After the probation officer left, the director asked Roy to go to the office with him to fill out an admission card. He replied to questions, simply and directly, with a slight smile. He was informed of the project's two inflexible rules—namely, that boys are not permitted to leave the grounds unless they are accompanied by an adult, nor are they permitted to converse with female patients at the Institute where they work. He replied that he understood these rules and laughed. When asked whether he had any questions, he said, "No, I don't. I've been waiting five weeks to come to Highfields at the Children's Home. I heard all about this place from the boys from Boston and from B. W——. If I think of anything, I'll ask questions." The director told him, also, that he was welcome to ask questions of any employee at the house at any time. He said, "One thing I'd like to do is to read those books you have. I'm interested in psychology." He was told he was welcome to do so. Then, he added, "My trouble is at home. I can't get along with my family, especially my mother. I think she hates me. I've been running away from home for a long time. I just can't seem to get along with my parents. I want to do something about it. I don't know if I can take it any longer." These remarks were made with intense feeling. He almost cried. The director said that perhaps the project could help him with his problem during his stay. Mr. L—— came in and took him out to give him a bed and bedding.

He set up his bed with the assistance of the K.P. boy, then Mr. L—— asked him to peel potatoes. After he completed this job, Mr. L—— gave him another one, along with the K.P. boy. It lasted until supper time. When the boys arrived from work, he came into the kitchen to assist the K.P. Some boys shouted, "Where's the new boy?" They saw him and went over to greet him, especially Bob. Roy sat down again and waited for supper. In the dining room he had a little difficulty finding a place to sit.

That evening, Roy went to bed at 10:00 P.M. and said "good night" to the director at bed check. At about 10:30 P.M., the director heard scuffling and loud talking, downstairs. As he walked down, he met Frank who said, "Mr. E——, that new boy won't come out of the bathroom, he's been there for a half hour already." The director told Frank to return to his bed. He then checked Roy's bed and found that it was wet near the pillow. The comforter and the rest of the bedding were dry. He got a dry sheet and placed it on the bed and returned upstairs. About twenty minutes later, he again heard noises downstairs. He went down and found Bill near the bathroom. Bill said, "I'd like to go to the toilet, that kid won't come out." When the director knocked on the door, Roy opened it slightly. The light was out. The director told him other boys wanted to use the toilet and asked if anything was wrong. He replied, "No, I'll be right out." After a few minutes, he came out and made his bed. There were no other incidents during the night.

It is a strange, bewildering world that confronts a boy when he arrives at Highfields. He has many thoughts about the house he will live in for the next few months of his life—some thoughts that are frightening, confusing, and even shocking; others that are hostile and rebellious. His initial perception of the Highfields social world will color his definition of the style of life at the project, and determines, in large measure, the kind of adjustment he will make during his first few weeks of residence. It will enter, however subtly, in the nature of the roles he will assume in his interpersonal relationships with his peers as well as with the adults in authority. It will play a large part in the degree to which he will be willing to get involved in the life of the project, both in its formal and informal aspects. For each boy, with variations, internalizes the values and norms of Highfields, and at the same time has an impact on it. Not only do boys relate with each other and with the authority figures, in terms of the customs and traditions which they find, but they also help to fashion new customs and new traditions.

The following excerpts from observations made by boys about

their initial conceptions of this social world indicate that they have a wide range of views. It is fairly common for new boys to be disturbed by their initial contact with Highfields because their expectations are shattered. By and large, their images of correctional institutions have been formed as a result of a brief period of residence in a local juvenile detention facility or by the descriptions of correctional institutions by their peers who have had experiences in them:

I thought I knew all about Highfields because I was in the Parental Home. When I came through the front door, the first thing I said to myself was, "This is a weird place." I expected somebody to meet me and shake my hand and wish me good luck. I was glad when all you did was to say hello. I didn't want anybody to wish me anything. After I got my bed made up and put my things away, I thought, "Now comes the bullshit. I'm going to get a lecture on how to be a good boy around here, what to do, what not to do and how to do it, to obey all the rules and that kind of crap." But instead, Mr. M—— came along and put me to work washing windows. I never did get that lecture. I'm glad because I wasn't in no mood to have anybody tell me what to do. But, to tell you the truth, I still think this is a weird place.

Often the boy's expectations of Highfields are based on rumors and misconceptions perpetrated by persons—peers and others—who want to reassure the boy that his stay away from home will be pleasant and tolerable:

I came up here for a vacation. I was told I was going to have my own room with a radio. I thought there was television and a swimming pool and no work. Just lay around, eat and go to town. I couldn't figure out why the judge wanted to send me to a place like that. But I wasn't going to say anything in court when he said I was going to Highfields. He told me it was going to help me, that it was different from a jail. But I didn't need any help, I just wanted to do my time. What a let-down when I got here. All I saw was a bunch of old beds, and when I found out that there was work to do, I said to myself, "This is no place for me."

In some instances a boy's conception is blurred by fear and extreme anxiety about his initiation into the peer-group life at Highfields:

I was scared shitless. I thought I was going to have to fight every boy here. I was trying to figure out how I was going to do it. I knew I couldn't fight all of the boys at the same time. I thought I could make it by fighting one boy each day. I wondered if I would last out because I wasn't going to be worth shit after that.

The notion is expressed occasionally that the informal, flexible, atmosphere and the absence of physical restraints such as walls, locks, bars, and custodians places an excessive responsibility on the boy, a responsibility he feels he cannot or does not want to bear. After walking around the house and talking with the K.P. boy for a few moments, a new boy came into the office and announced:

I'm not going to make it here. It's too free. I just walked around and didn't see any fence or guards. I want to go back to the county jail. I'd rather spend a year locked up in jail than I would living here for four months. I don't want to be free. I don't want to worry about problems. I just want to be locked up, so I can do my time and get out. I'm not going to make it here. I know I'll run away or do something that's going to get me in a lot of trouble.

Less frequently, a contrary view is encountered. Just as the car in which he arrived pulled out of the driveway and was out of sight, a new boy came into the office and shouted angrily:

You can't keep me here. This is a jail. The lady told me I was going to have a lot of freedom, but there's no freedom here. I'm a singer. I like to go to dances and night clubs where there are a lot of dames. There are no dames here. I gotta have at least three dates a week. I can support my self by singing. I'll go crazy here. I'm not going to stay here.

Sometimes, the stable, sophisticated, gang delinquent formulates plans to deal with the situation here in a simple, forthright manner:

When I heard I was coming here, I made plans to run away the day I got here. I was going to have one of my boys meet me at the first gate with his car. Then, at night, after everybody was in bed, I'd walk down and meet him. We'd go home to get some clothes and money and go south. I knew where we could get a job in Florida. I felt I should run away because I heard it was so easy.

Seriously disturbed boys prejudge the situation here and outline their strategy for dealing with it largely in terms of hostile
resistence:

I hated this place when I came here. I hated you and everybody that
worked here. I thought this place was a nut house, and you were a
psychologist or a psychiatrist who was trying to find out if I was crazy.
Then, after I came to my first meeting, I knew I wasn't going to like it.
I thought the judge really had it in for me to send me to a place like
this. I didn't give a shit about problems. I didn't have any problems.
I never heard of problems before. Not only that, I didn't even know
what a problem was. I wasn't going to say anything in the meetings. I
was just going to set there and do my time until you sent me home.

There are other types of resistance which are expressed. A more
extreme type was exhibited by a boy who managed to delay his
arrival at Highfields:

One day the probation officer called my house and told my mother to
drive me up here. But I talked her into letting me go with my buddy,
in his car. When we got to the first gate, I wouldn't get out of the car.
He told me to stay but I said he'd have to drag me out of the car and
dump me. So we turned around and went home. I told my mother we got
lost and couldn't find the place. I didn't tell the probation officer about
it. I thought if I got a job, he'd forget about it. But he didn't. When he
found out I was home, he drove me up himself.

More recently, as an increasing number of people become fa-
miliar with the program here, more balanced and objective views
are expressed:

I knew what Highfields was all about even before I went to court.
Maybe you guys think I'm throwing some shit, but I remember thinking that if I got into trouble, this is the one place I wanted to be sent.
You see, some of my buddies were here. I saw how it straightened them
out. To tell the truth, when I thought of all the fights I was getting into
and the trouble I was having with my family, I wanted to be straightened
out too, the way my friends were. But don't get me wrong, I didn't get
into this trouble just to get sent here. I'm not that crazy. But, I knew
I'd have to be straightened out sooner or later. Don't laugh, but I'm
glad I finally got caught.

Sometimes, parents and friends are so fearful that the boy will run away or refuse to go to Highfields, that they deliberately deceive him. They feel that the main task is to get the boy to Highfields and that, once he arrives, the authorities will be able to deal with him:

My parents and even my brother told me I was going to stay only two weeks. My probation officer said I'd be here for three or four months. But, on the way up here, my brother and my father kept telling me that I'd be out in two weeks if I cooperated. They said I was sent here just to find out why I got into so much trouble, then you would send a report to the judge and I'd be sent home. I think maybe they thought I'd run away if I discovered I'd be here about four months. I guess I should've listened to my probation officer.

Occasionally, after a very brief and cursory investigation of the program, a boy decides that his offense is a very minor one which does not really warrant being placed in an institution. Therefore, he decides that the judge made a hasty decision which he would be willing to reconsider if he were supplied with the "real facts" in the case. The boy feels that the only wise course of action is to request another court appearance and, of course, the opportunity to acquaint the judge with the proper evidence. Generally, these boys are "apron-string delinquents" who are frightened by the appearance and the mannerisms of the other boys:

I want to go back to court because the judge made a mistake in my case. I'm different from the other boys around here. They're all thieves and hoodlums. I never stole anything in my life. I'm not a thief. I had a little trouble at home with my father. We just never got along that's all. I thought about the whole thing at the Parental Home. I've learned my lesson. I know I can get along with my father now.

In many instances, probation officers, particularly when they drive the boy to the house, go to great lengths to help the boy understand the nature of the Highfields social world. As a result, many boys do not have misconceptions about the program:

My probation officer explained all about this place. He told me about the group meetings and the work on the farm. I knew about going to town and getting furloughs. I didn't want to come here but he made

me realize that I was lucky to come here, especially after the judge gave
me a suspended sentence to the reformatory.

In general, however, personal evaluations are paramount in the
boys' conceptions of Highfields. They persist, despite attempts by
the various judges and their probation officers, as indicated in the
preceeding illustration to properly orient the boys and prepare
them for residence. These impressions reveal the range of feelings
that any group of deliquent boys might have as they prepare to
meet a new social world, a correctional world, in which they may
have little or no motivation to play a part.

The origins of the correctional world described above are difficult to trace, for it is like an idea which is compounded from still
other ideas, each with a history of its own. We must satisfy ourselves with selecting a point in time and accepting it as the period
in the development of a particular notion, plan, or program which
assists us in understanding the idea and in tracing the course of
its movement. The well of the past is deep, so deep that it is pre-
carious and even misleading to point to a single event as the moment of the conception of any idea. And so it is with Highfields.
Although it began operations in the summer of 1950, it did not
emerge full-blown. Not only was it several years in the making,
but it has its antecedents in the various developments that have
taken place in the correctional world in recent years.

One of these developments in the United States has been the
establishment of relatively small, open facilities especially for the
treatment of youthful offenders. The privately endowed institutions for the treatment of emotionally disturbed children [1] have
been in the forefront of this movement which had its origins in
Europe. Recently, however, the state correctional systems have
joined this movement by setting up camp and forestry programs
for small groups of inmates, usually as part of a pre-release program. The Highfields program is part and parcel of this development, but it encompasses some features which are at variance

---

[1] In a survey conducted in 1951, the United States Children's Bureau listed 36
facilities for the treatment of children, both public and private, in its direc-
tory, *Residential Treatment Centers for Emotionally Disturbed Children.* U.S.
Gov't. Printing Office: Washington, D. C., 1953.

with the conventional type of publicly supported correctional programs for youthful offenders.

One of these features is the guided group interaction aspect of Highfields. In this regard it is possible to trace the influence of a new and relatively successful treatment method which envolved around the work of Dr. Pratt at the turn of the century, namely the use of "conversational groups." This approach, referred to in the literature as the class method, was modified and expanded to include the treatment of other maladjusted persons.[2] The group psychotherapy movement, as it is generally referred to now, was expanded greatly during the Second World War. Because trained personnel were in short supply, while military casualties increased as the war continued, group psychotherapy received a tremendous impetus in the armed services. The effectiveness of group psychotherapy in processing delinquent soldiers who were sent to rehabilitation centers was sufficiently impressive for it to become an integral part of the rehabilitation programs of all military correctional installations. The system was utilized as an attempt at mass therapy of these soldiers in hopes of restoring them to duty.[3] After the end of the war, Dr. F. Lovell Bixby, Director of Correction and Parole, brought Dr. McCorkle, who had participated in this program, to New Jersey to set up a group therapy program in the state correctional system. Later, Dr. McCorkle went to Highfields as the director, to establish the program which centered around a form of group therapy, namely, guided group interaction.

---

[2] J. H. Pratt, "The Class Method of Treating Consumption in the Homes of the Poor," *Journal of the American Medical Association*, August 31, 1907.

[3] Joseph Abrahams and Lloyd W. McCorkle, "Group Psychotherapy of Military Offenders," *American Journal of Sociology*, Vol. 51, No. 5, March 1946, pp. 455–464.

Joseph Abrahams and Lloyd W. McCorkle, "Group Psychotherapy at an Army Rehabilitation Center," *Journal of Nervous Diseases*, February 1947.

More especially, the Highfields program is indebted to the group psychotherapy program developed at the 5th Service Command Army Rehabilitation Center at Fort Knox, Kentucky, commanded by Colonel A. Miller under whose supportive understanding Dr. Alexander Wolf was able to initiate a group treatment program embracing a total correctional population. This program was subsequently expanded and modified by Lipkin, McCorkle, and Abrahams.

It can be seen, then, that Highfields, which was officially referred to as the New Jersey Experimental Project for the Treatment of Youthful Offenders, has its roots in the developments
which have emerged in the fields of correction over the past years.
Unlike many other comparable correctional facilities which were
designed to attack the problems of young offenders, Highfields
has become deeply rooted in the state correctional system. This
is largely a consequence of the circumstances of its establishment.

For over thirty years before Highfields was envisioned, the New
Jersey Department of Institutions and Agencies was well known
for seeking new methods of meeting its responsibilities in the fields
of correction, mental health, and welfare. Innovations were accepted as necessary for progress. The public, in general, because
of a broad program of citizen participation in the management
and direction of departmental activities, understood and accepted
innovations.

Early in 1947, under the immediate direction of Dr. Bixby,
Lloyd W. McCorkle inaugurated programs of "guided group interaction" in the correctional institutions. The value of these
programs was recognized, and by the time Highfields, with its
strong emphasis on "group" was proposed, the policy makers,
fiscal authorities, and courts did not have to be convinced of the
soundness of the basic technique. These two facts made the Highfields idea "make sense" when it was first suggested.

On February 16, 1950, the Department of Institutions and
Agencies was notified that the New York Foundation had voted
a grant of $12,500 per year for two years. This grant, together
with a later generous gift by Mr. and Mrs. Douglas H. MacNeil
of Princeton, assured the operation of Highfields for two years.

As these developments were in progress, the Vincent Astor
Foundation, through a special sub-committee of Mr. Barklie
Henry and Mr. William Jackson, had appointed a Scientific Advisory Committee to consider the research proposal. Professor
Ernest W. Burgess of the University of Chicago accepted the
chairmanship, and Mr. G. Howland Shaw, Professor Walter Reckless of Ohio State University, and Dr. Richard L. Jenkins of the

Veterans Administration accepted membership. Dr. Quinter Holsopple, Professor Wellman Warner, and Dr. Lloyd McCorkle were subsequently added to the Committee.

During June, 1950, preparations were begun to make the house ready for occupancy. A detail of twenty inmates from the State Reformatory at Annandale Farms who were eligible for parole two to six weeks after their arrival at Highfields opened the project and functioned as a housekeeping detail. Minor structural changes were under way in the house. Shower stalls and washroom facilities were installed for use by the boys.

There was a minimum of equipment in the house, and much of it was obsolete. War surplus sources provided desks for the office, beds, and chairs for the dining room. The dining room tables, the refrigerator, dishware, and other items were secondhand equipment, but they were sturdy and in usable condition. Some of these items were replaced after the State took over the project. The houskeeping detail cleaned the house, painted the rooms, cleared some of the boulders in back of the house to provide a small recreation area, and assisted with the cooking. The staff consisted of Dr. Lloyd W. McCorkle as director and Mr. Joseph Lyons as caretaker. Later a secretary and cottage parents were added.

On July 12, 1950, the first probationer arrived from the Essex County Juvenile Court. With the admission of this boy, the Highfields program was formally launched. Shortly thereafter, other boys began arriving and the reformatory inmates began leaving. During this interim period the first guided group interaction sessions were held. The members of the first therapy group at the project were the progenitors of a culture and a style of life that has emerged and developed through the years at Highfields. Today when a boy arrives, he enters into, and eventually becomes an integral part of, an ongoing social system.

The Highfields project, which has its origins in the mainstream of modern penology, was made possible through the collaborative efforts and energies of many groups and individuals: the Division of Correction and Parole of the New Jersey Department of Institutions and Agencies, the members of the State Board of Control, the various judges and their probation departments of the State of New Jersey, the New York Foundation, and the Vincent Astor Foundation.

After two years of operation under the joint auspices of the State of New Jersey and the New York Foundation, Highfields was formally admitted into the Department of Institutions and Agencies as a part of the New Jersey correctional system. On July 1, 1952, the State assumed full control and responsibility for the project.

II

A Typical Day at Highfields

IN ORDER TO PROVIDE AN OVERALL PICTURE OF THE FLOW OF LIFE at Highfields, we present below a description of a typical day. It is not possible to describe all of the activities of all the boys and staff members during any single day. We intend only to give the reader a panoramic view of what may happen to the people who live and work at Highfields in the course of a day. The events which are portrayed were selected from the experiences of various people covering a period of several weeks.

At 5:30 A.M., Mr. M——, the cottage supervisor, came down and opened the kitchen door. He prepared the coffee for breakfast. Then, he walked upstairs to the small room to wake Bill who was assigned as K.P. for the day. He shook Bill and called him. Bill sat up and yawned. He shook his head and rubbed his eyes. Slowly, he shifted around until he was sitting on the edge of his bed. Then, he got up and dressed. After washing, he went downstairs. By this time, Mrs. M——, the cook, was in the kitchen preparing breakfast. As Bill walked in, he said, "Hello, Mom, what are we having?" She replied, "Good morning, Bill. We're having eggs, be sure to put out the flat plates, too." Bill went into the dining room to set the table. At 6:00 A.M., Mr. M—— began his tour of the boys' rooms. He went to each bed and tried to awaken each boy. Some boys jumped up and began to dress, others grumbled and muttered and tried to get more rest. Frank and John, who slept in the big room upstairs, jumped back into bed as soon as Mr. M—— left their room. Gary said, "You guys better get up, Mr. M——'ll be back in a minute. He'll give you

the pit." John said, "Hell he will." He got up again. Frank made
no reply for he had fallen asleep. Warren, the fourth boy in the
room, was dressed and washed. He began sweeping the room and
emptying ash trays. It was his turn to keep the room clean. John
grabbed his pillow and hit Frank on the head several times saying, "Get up, you sleepy bastard. You've been sleeping your way
through Highfields for two months now. Wake up, wake up."
Frank tried to protect himself. Gary, who was standing at the
door, ran into the room and said, "Here comes M——. Get Frank
up." At this announcement, Frank swiftly moved out of bed and
bent down pretending he was putting on his shoes and cursing
them at the same time. Mr. M—— stepped into the room and
said, "Come on Frank, you'll be late for breakfast." John and
Gary began laughing at Frank. John said, "He'll get your ass yet."
Frank stood up and rubbed his eyes. Then he stumbled over to
his locker and mumbled "F— you, John." By this time, Warren
had finished sweeping the floor and had picked up the waste
paper basket. He took it downstairs to empty it. John and Gary
grabbed their towels and headed for the washroom, leaving Frank
alone.

This scene, and others similar to it, was being repeated in each
of the other three rooms where the boys slept.

In the washroom, the dominant activity was noise making.
Some boys were singing, others were busily washing, still others
were conversing, especially Harry. He loved to talk and this morning, like every morning, Harry cornered one or more boys and
regaled them with his stories, his complaints, his plans and his
experiences. Steve, who was always needling Harry, said, "Harry,
you'll be still talking when you crawl into your grave. I'll bet
you'll be asking questions when you hit the pearly gates. Saint
Pete won't have a chance." Harry replied laughingly, "Saint Peter
hell. Didn't I tell you. I made arrangements already with the
devil. I'm going to be his right-hand man. I'm going to advise
him about who to take and who not to take. You'll be down
there with Steve, and the first thing we're going to do is to roast
your balls." Some of the others who were listening to this exchange burst into laughter. Steve swung his towel at Harry who

ducked out of the way. Then he chased Harry out of the room. In another corner, Tony was complaining, "Another day, another fifty cents. I hate to get up around here. Work, work, work. More weeds to pick. If I ever see another weed after I leave Highfields, I'm going to save it, so I can ram it down F——'s throat. That guy thinks the most important thing in the world is a goddamn weed." Dick, who was standing next to Tony, said, "Fifty cents a day hell. If you were paid for every weed you picked you'd starve to death. You never worked a day in your life, not even around here. When you get paid on Saturday, it's like stealing." Tony, who was drying his face, replied angrily, "Listen to hot rod here. Since when did you become a worker?" Dick said, "Since I came here, so what's it to you?" This interplay was interrupted by the sound of the bell in the kitchen announcing that breakfast was ready. There was a mad scramble to get out of the washroom, except for Frank, who was leisurely combing his hair. Some boys had washed earlier and were waiting outside the dining room. The others thundered downstairs and raced through the kitchen. As John ran past the washroom, he yelled, "Frank, get the lead out." Without turning his head, Frank said, "Yeah, yeah."

It was 6:30 A.M. Downstairs the boys were lined up outside the dining room while Mr. M—— counted them. He said that somebody was missing as Frank strolled out of the kitchen and got into line. John and Gary began laughing at Frank who smiled back, while glancing at Mr. M——. Then, Mrs. M—— came in and said, "Okay boys." They dashed into the dining room and noisily distributed themselves among three tables, six boys to a table. They were followed by Mr. M—— who sat at the fourth table. As usual, Frank had difficulty finding a seat. John yelled, "Hey, Frank, over here, we saved the hot seat just for you." The other boys laughed at Frank, who was visibly embarrassed. Just as the boys were finishing their cereal, Mrs. M—— came in with a tray of eggs and distributed them on the plates. At varying times, several boys yelled to the K.P. for additional supplies of bread, butter and jelly.

During the meal, the boys were engaged in noisy conversation. As each boy finished his meal, he gathered together his dishes

and silverware and carried them into the kitchen. There he distributed each item into separate piles. In the kitchen, Bill, the
K.P., was eating his breakfast and talking with Mrs. M——. After
breakfast the boys went back to their rooms to make their beds,
clean their rooms, and get ready to go to work. Downstairs in the
big room, Harry asked Steve if he would walk down the road with
him to meet the truck. In this way, they would be able to get seats
in the cab of the truck. The two boys got into their jackets and
prepared to leave. Just as they got to the door, Harry turned and
addressed the boys who were present, "Listen, you mother f——,
I left a pack of cigarettes in my locker, I expect it to be there
when I get back tonight." Tom yelled back, "You can't remember
the last time you bought a pack of cigarettes. You're the biggest
moocher at Highfields." Harry smiled as he replied, "Man, I
didn't say I bought the pack." Then he left, as Steve was urging
him to get moving. They passed through the kitchen and paused
to talk with Mrs. M——. There were several other boys leaning
against the sink and the table near the window in the kitchen.
Harry said, "Hey, Mom, we're going down the road, got any mail
to go out?" She said, "Harry, I don't believe you. You'll never get
past the bend in the road." Harry laughed as he walked out with
Steve. When they passed the small room downstairs, Harry stepped
in and asked Larry for a cigarette. Larry said that he had only
three and he was saving them for the rest of the day. Harry began
talking in his usual smooth, easy, convincing manner. He threatened, he cajoled, he joked until he succeeded in getting one.
Then he sniffed it, smiled, and put it in his pocket as he walked
out of the room. It was about 7:00 A.M. and Mr. L—— was just
arriving. He came through the door and said, "Hi boys." Then
he went into the kitchen. As he passed the small room downstairs
he heard Larry arguing with the Professor. The latter boy was
saying, "Why don't you get some good music on that damn radio.
All I ever hear is the Mombo and the Congo, that goddamn Bop
and the Ran-Tan. I'm getting sick of it, day and night. One of
these days I'm gonna bust that radio on your head." Larry replied
angrily, "Listen, Professor, any time you wanna move out of this
room go tell Mr. E——. It's crowded in here as it is. Besides,
you're a pain in the ass with that locker. Painting it, scrubbing it,

cleaning it, looking after it like it was a broad. I'm getting out of that locker soon." The Professor retorted, "Right now is too soon. Where the hell were you brought up, in a pig sty?" Tom, who was lying on his bed yelled down, "Why don't you guys shut up. I'm trying to finish this letter to my girl. I can't hear myself think." The Professor shouted back, "Look boy, forget that dame. How do you know she's not two-timing you? There're a lot of fish in the pond waiting to be hooked. You'll be joining the High-fields Bachelors Club soon. Look what happened to Steve and Jerry. They're charter members." Tom glowered back, "Cut it boy, cut it." Outside, the truck pulled up driven by Mr. F——, the work supervisor. He blew the horn and came into the kitchen. There he greeted Mrs. M——, Mr. L—— and several boys who were standing around talking. Tom came into the kitchen and, addressing no one in particular, asked, "Say, who's mailman today?" Tony, who was standing closest to him, yelled, "Jerry, the new boy." Tom left. Then, Mr. F—— said, "Well, I guess we'd better get going. Okay boys, let's go." He waved to the adults in the room. As he left, he was followed by the boys. Some of them came running down the stairs, others rushed out of the big room. Almost all of them had made attempts to straighten out their ruffled beds. When Mr. F—— reached the truck, Harry and Steve were seated in the cab taunting some of the other boys who were climbing on the back. Mr. F—— waited behind the truck until the boys climbed on it. He asked if everyone was present. John said, "Yeah, everybody but Frank and here he comes. Hey, Frank, shake it up." Frank slowly approached the truck trying to ignore the sarcastic comments that were tossed at him by the other boys. The boys pulled him up on the truck. Then he turned to John and said, "Why don't you cut the shit, John?" John merely laughed at him. He was joined by some of the other boys. Then Mr. F——walked to the cab, entered, and drove off. He stopped the truck at the end of the lane. Tony yelled at Jerry and said, "Hey new boy mail the letters." Jerry collected the mail and deposited it in the box. The truck started for the Neuro-Psychiatric Institute about five miles away, where the boys work each day. It was 7:30 A.M.

In the house, Bill, the K.P., had finished washing the dishes.

He was starting on another of a series of jobs including cleaning the office, dining room, and downstairs bathroom, sweeping and mopping the hall, pantry and kitchen floors, cleaning the washroom and showers, sweeping and dusting the back stairway and back hall, cleaning out the garage, taking the garbage out to the pit and covering it with dirt, setting the table for lunch, doing the lunch dishes and pots, cleaning and peeling potatoes, and setting the table for dinner before the boys returned from work at 5:00 P.M.

The truck pulled up to the storehouse of the Institute at 7:50 A.M. John and Gary, who worked in the butcher shop, were dropped off. Then the truck swung around and went to the barn where the remainder of the boys received their work assignments. Mr. F—— assigned Mario, the Professor, and Warren to work on the trash detail. This detail is supervised by an employee of the Institute. Mario, very sheepishly, approached Mr. F——. He asked if Larry could replace him on the garbage detail. Mr. F—— said that he could not. Mario turned and shook his head at Larry. Mr. P——, the Institute employee in charge of the truck garden, assigned the boys the job of filling burlap bags with squash piled in one corner of a shed. Most of the boys teamed up in groups: Midget with Whitey; Larry, Steve, and Harry; Tom with Mike. Frank volunteered to tie the sacks after they were filled. Mike immediately found a seat. He put the squash in a bag held by Tom, picking them up with one hand and very sleepily talking to Joe. Midget moved to the back of the shed with Whitey, where they worked together. The triad immediately got involved in aimless conversation. Frank was having a difficult time tying the sacks, so Mr. P—— asked Steve to help him. Harry immediately went over with Steve and the three of them had a discussion about techniques used to tie bags. Midget examined the situation, then he came over and informed them of the correct technique. Steve went back to work with Larry, and Midget returned to Whitey. For the duration of this job, the boys remained in this arrangement.

Throughout this assignment, Mike and Tom worked painfully and slowly. Whitey spent most of the time looking around, while

Frank worked feverishly. At about 9:30 this job was completed and they waited for the next assignment until the return of Mr. P——, who had left with some of the boys. All the boys draped themselves over bags of squash except Steve, who walked across the road and sat down on a pile of cement blocks. Shortly thereafter, Harry walked over and sat down next to him. They became involved in a long discussion regarding card games, old friends in N——, and their experiences before coming to Highfields.

About a half hour later, Mr. P—— returned and explained that the boys would have to pick beans, and drove them to the field, approximately a half mile away.

Each boy took a basket and began working. It wasn't long before Midget and Mike were far out front while Tom, Harry, and Steve lagged far behind. In fact, the latter three boys sat on baskets and slowly and deliberately picked beans one at a time. Larry became involved in a race with Mike, Whitey spoke to no one but occasionally would stand and stare into space for five or ten minutes at a time. Sometimes he would pick up a bean and look at it and then toss it casually into his basket. Midget was very diligently picking beans which he threw on the ground. He would then pick up the beans that he had dropped and place them in his basket. Everyone else placed the beans in a basket as they picked them. Occasionally, they would ask each other how many baskets they had filled. Harry became quite loud in his discussion with Steve. Mr. F—— told him to make less noise. He did for a while, but later he resumed his loud talking.

At 11:30 they went to eat lunch near the greenhouse. Mike asked if the boys could go to the store for ice cream and sodas. Mr. F—— said not until Mr. P—— returned from lunch. The boys took their sandwiches and dispersed around the area.

After some jockeying around the boys ended up in three small groups: Roger, Frank, Moose, Walter, Professor, and Whitey in one group; Harry, Willie, Larry, Dan, and Jerry in a second group; Midget, Pete, John, Tony, Mario, Mike, Tom, and Dick in a third group. The latter group concentrated their efforts on hazing Tom. Some of the boys threw away their sandwiches without eating them. John very loudly stated: When are they going to quit giving us this shit? You'd think they would put some jelly on the peanut butter." Midget tried to explain there wasn't any jelly at the project. However, John continued to curse the sandwiches. Harry yelled over to Mr. F—— and asked whether or not he liked the sandwiches. When he replied he didn't, Harry said, "Now you see what we have to put up with day after day."

Mr. F—— told him that he knew about the situation and that he would probably have to put up with it for as long as he was at Highfields.

At 12:30, Mr. P—— returned from his lunch. Mr. F—— took two boys to the store to buy ice cream and soda. After they returned they distributed the ice cream and soda and all the boys returned to the farm and continued to pick beans.

Harry worked alongside of Steve. They began talking about their delinquent experiences in N——. Steve explained, "The best way to steal an overcoat in a department store is to walk in with an empty coat box, take the coat and put it in the box and walk out." He said he had tried this technique successfully in several locations.

Harry retorted, "Only an amateur would do that. I used to steal a lot of stuff from B——'s where I worked, by signing in early with some fake name and picking the stuff up that I wanted and putting it in the bag and walking out of a door where I knew there wasn't a detective posted. Then after I stashed the stuff I'd go to work in the basement." Whitey worked by himself. Occasionally he would stare at the sky or count the beans in his hand. Tom picked beans even more slowly than he had during the morning. After a while he began to inquire about how many more bushels would have to be picked. He walked to the end of the rows, counted the bushels that had been picked, and began a discussion with Midget about the quota of bushels to be picked by each boy.

At about 2:30 Mr. F—— returned and assigned the next job, which involved picking corn and placing it in bags. At 4 o'clock, Mr. F—— gave the boys a break and they sat together on top of the bags of corn. Their discussion involved a criticism of Highfields employees. At 4:30 Mr. P—— returned with the truck and the remaining boys. Everyone got on the truck to return to High-fields.

As the truck approached the Highfields lane, the arguing and singing in the back became noisier. As the truck pulled into the yard, most of the boys were singing very loudly. When the truck stopped they climbed down, dashed into the house, ran through the kitchen, and headed for the office. The group milled around the office door asking for mail. Only four boys received letters. Harry asked, "How about me, no mail?" When he learned that there were no letters for him, he turned and walked away saying, "Damn it, that bitch better put up soon." Tom, who was opening his letter, said, "Forget it, Harry." Harry smiled and remarked, "Oh, well, I'd better scratch her ass. She ain't gonna do me no good anyway."

Some of the boys returned to their rooms to rest before shower-ing, others stopped off to talk, a few paused in the kitchen to ask Mrs. M—— about supper. Mr. F—— was in the kitchen talking with Tom. Tom wanted to know how Mr. F—— felt about his chances for going home. Upstairs, Larry, Steve, and Tony were taking a shower. Tony was imitating an opera singer while the other boys tried to shout him down. Bill was busily setting the table and bringing in the plates.

At 5:30 P.M., Bill rang the bell announcing that supper was ready. There was a rush for the dining room. Willie was first in line, trying to prevent some of the other boys from getting in the dining room ahead of him. He took off his cap and threw it on a chair. He said, half in jest, "That's where the King sits." While Mr. M—— walked down the line to see if all the boys were present, Frank strolled in from the kitchen. Mrs. M—— came in and said, "Okay, Jim, we're all set." The boys rushed into the dining room and sat down. Mr. M——, Mr. and Mrs. E—— (the director and his wife) and their son walked in behind them and sat at one table. Almost all of the boys were seated in the same chairs they had occupied at breakfast. After the initial outburst, the boys quieted down and conversed in moderate tones. When most of the boys had finished eating, Mrs. M—— came in and reminded Harry that it was his turn to clean the dining room.

He said, "Okay Ma, I'll be ready in a minute." He continued talking to Steve until all the boys except Tom departed. Tom was sitting alone at his table smoking a cigarette and staring at the wall. Bill came in and urged Harry to get the plates and left-overs off the tables so that he could finish the dishes. Harry merely nodded his head. Soon afterward, he arose and left with Steve. Tom followed them. Harry returned with a tray and began clearing the tables. In the kitchen, Jerry was cleaning the pots. It was now 6:15 P.M.

The phone rang. It was a call for Tom. Mr. E—— called him. Outside, some boys were playing basketball, other boys were lying on their beds, some of them were listening to the radio, while others just talked.

At 7:00 P.M. the boys in the first meeting came into the office at varying intervals, until seven boys were present. Roger, Mike, and Larry did not attend this session. The boys seated themselves in a semicircle against the sides of the room. In the center, Mr. E—— was seated at his desk.

Tom began the meeting when he asked if the group felt he was ready to go home. He reviewed his career at Highfields, pointing out that he felt he had learned many things he never thought he could learn. After this summary he turned to the group and asked, "How does the group think I'll make out when I leave Highfields?" "What about it, Professor, you always have something to say." The Professor expressed his feelings and so did the other boys as follows:

The Professor: "There are two things Tom has to do to make out on probation. He has to get a job first, then he has to get married. If he gets a job and doesn't get married he'll drift back to his old ways. The same thing will happen to him if he gets married and tries to let his wife support him. He needs both of them, not just one of 'em."

Dick: "I think Tom's chances of staying out of trouble are 80-20. I think he can stay away from his old friends. But there is still a chance he might take up drinking again, but he'll know when to stop."

Tony: "I don't think Tom will get into trouble again if he stays away from the gang. I think Tom has wised up. He knows he'll end up as a Bowery bum if he isn't careful. Tom has to decide which side of the street he wants to stay on. He can stay with his girl friend and sit home and maybe watch T.V. or he can go across the street and go with his buddies. But I don't think he'll cross that street."

Harry: "I don't think Tom will get into trouble. But he does have to watch himself. I agree with the Professor. I think Tom should get married, after he saves some money."

Steve: "Well, I think Tom's chances are 50-50. Second, I think Tom knows what he wants to do. If he wants to go with his boys, then he'll go. He doesn't need anybody to coax him or tell him to go. If Tom wants to go with his girl friend, then he'll go with her. It's all up to Tom."

Jerry: (Jerry offered no comment regarding Tom's adjustment on probation. He merely shook his head.)

Tom: "I'm not saying that I'm not going to get into trouble. I don't really know. I have to get out of Highfields to find that out. But I will say this much, I know what I'm going to do to stay out of trouble. I'm going to take a drink, yeah. I know I'll do that. I know I'm going to see some of my buddies and if one of them gets into a fight, I don't know exactly what I'll do. I mean, if it's just a little fight, okay, but if he got hit with a bottle, then I'm not sure what I'll do. I'm not depending on any girl to keep me out of trouble, but I'm going to ask her to help me. I know I'll need that help, otherwise it's all up to me."

Mr. E—— summarized the comments of the group. Then he announced that Tom would be going home on Friday morning. Tom sat up in his chair and smiled. Harry, Tony, and the Professor congratulated him. After the meeting ended, the boys arose and began walking out of the office. Before Tom left, Mr. E—— handed him an envelope containing a blank sheet of paper. Tom said, "What do you think I ought to write down?" Mr. E—— replied, "Put down whatever you want to." Tom nodded his head and said, "'Okay,'" and walked out.

It was 8:30 P.M. and the boys who were members of the second group began coming in. While this group was having its meeting, the boys in the first group scattered throughout the house. Tom lay down on Larry's bed and listened to the radio. Tony was in the dining room writing a letter to his girl friend. The Professor and Harry were drinking milk and eating jelly sandwiches which they had made in the kitchen. Steve joined them later and shared in the food. Jerry and Dick took a walk down the lane.

At 9:50 the boys in the second group came out of the office. Everyone prepared to go to bed. At 10:00 P.M., Mr. E—— walked from room to room talking with the boys, making bed check, and turning out the lights. At approximately 11:00 P.M., Mr. E—— went through the house again, making a second bed check. In one room he told Larry to turn down the radio. Also, he told the Professor to be careful about smoking in bed. By 11:30 P.M. everyone was sleeping.

———————

This picture of a day at Highfields reflects the daily schedule which is presented below and points up the three main features of the program—namely, the work situation, contacts with the community, and the guided group interaction sessions.

An average weekday in the life of a boy at Highfields is described below.

>   6:00– 6:30 A.M.—arise
>   6:30– 7:00 A.M.—breakfast
>   7:00– 7:30 A.M.—clean up rooms and make beds
>   7:30 A.M.—depart for Institute
>   8:00–12:00 M. —Institute work assignments
>   12:00– 1:00 P.M.—lunch
>   1:00– 4:30 P.M.—Institute work assignments
>   4:30 P.M.—leave Institute
>   5:00– 5:30 P.M.—prepare for dinner
>   5:30– 6:30 P.M.—dinner
>   7:00– 8:30 P.M.—guided group interaction sessions,
>   first group
>   8:30–10:00 P.M.—guided group interaction sessions,
>   second group
>   10:15 P.M.—lights out

On Saturdays, the boys clean the house in the morning and they have outdoor recreation in the afternoon. Also, they have an opportunity to go to town with an employee to make purchases and to get haircuts. After receiving their weekly wages in the evening, the entire group, accompanied by an employee, goes to surrounding towns to attend movies, go to stores, and make phone calls. On Sunday, breakfast is at 9:00 A.M., after which all boys are free to go to a church of their own choice in town under the supervision of an employee. On Sunday afternoon, visits start at 12:00 noon and end at 7:00 P.M. The boys are free to leave the project with their visitors as long as an adult is included in the party.

WORK SITUATION

As indicated above, all the boys except the K.P. boy work as quasi-employees at a nearby state hospital for forty hours a week, usually as farm laborers. In return for their work, they receive fifty cents each day. Also, clothing is issued for work details by Highfields, although most of the clothes worn by the boys are supplied by their families.

A large and important part of each boy's daily life is the work that he performs at this hospital. To many of these boys, who have begun to internalize a delinquent style of life, work has a low social value. It is regarded with contempt or it is viewed as inimical to their best interests. Since "only suckers work," these boys come to Highfields with little or no desire for steady, full-time work and without substantial training and experience in work situations.

Perhaps the most difficult adjustment a boy must make during his first days at Highfields is adjustment to this situation. This is so because the work program has been set up to approximate, as nearly as possible, a work situation a boy might find in the community. And since, in almost every instance, work is defined as conventional behavior, immediately it becomes a problem for each boy.

The work program at Highfields is organized in the following manner:

As indicated earlier, each boy receives fifty cents each day that he works. Also, he is subject to disciplinary measures which may be invoked by the work supervisor, or by an employee of the Institute who may be supervising him. For example, a boy may be suspended for a few days or he may be fired. In these instances, the boy is assigned to duties at Highfields; he does not, however, receive any remuneration for these services. Since the boys work at a State institution, they come into daily contact with adults other than those employed at Highfields, and they are faced with the responsibility of maintaining acceptable relationships with them.

At the same time, each boy must cooperate with his peers, who will be judging him in terms of such factors as whom he selects as a work partner, his work habits, the manner in which he gets along with his supervisor, and the way in which he accepts or rejects the rules for membership in the peer group. Later, an important factor is the realization that the work situation provides many of the experiences and feelings he and his fellow group members will discuss in the nightly guided group interaction sessions.

At the Institute, each day, three boys are assigned to the garbage collection detail under the supervision of an employee of the Institute; two boys are assigned to the butcher shop under the supervision of the head butcher, and the remainder of the boys are assigned to the farm detail.

Entries from the work record which are cited below illustrate the types and amount of work performed by the farm detail:

September 14th—Picked and delivered 140 baskets of tomatoes, 24 baskets of squash and 80 bags of cabbage.
September 15th—Racked up 217 baskets of tomatoes, delivered 15 baskets of cabbage, 40 baskets of beets, 40 baskets of tomatoes, unloaded 15 tons of feed and picked up empty bags and baskets at the cottages.

CONTACTS WITH THE COMMUNITY

Within limits, the boys in residence are granted a wide range of opportunities to keep in touch with the conventional world.

These opportunities are not regarded as privileges, as they are in a typical correctional facility. Rather, they are rights to which every boy is entitled, regardless of who he is or when he arrived, for they belong to the group as a whole. Outside of the work situation, the major types of contact with the community are three-day furloughs and trips to nearby towns to attend movies, church, etc.

During their stay at the project, all boys receive two or more three-day furloughs from Friday morning to Sunday evening to visit their families and contact their probation officers. The boy leaves the project alone or in the company of other boys who are also on furlough. He returns without official help or summons. During the past five years, several hundred furloughs were granted, and in only four cases were the conditions of the furlough violated. On all national holidays except Christmas, Easter, and Thanksgiving, the boys are free to receive visits from their families and friends from 12:00 noon to 7:00 P.M. On Christmas, Easter, and Thanksgiving, all boys receive three or four-day furloughs. There are no restrictions on the number of visits a boy may receive or on the persons who may visit him. In addition, the boys are permitted to leave the project to attend weddings, graduations, and to visit seriously ill relatives.

There is no type of censorship, either of mail, movies, radio, newspapers, or magazines at Highfields. Such censorship would be inconsistent with the basic philosophy of the project.

All new boys have heard about furloughs prior to their arrival. However, they do not always have a clear conception of the number of furloughs that are granted nor of the procedure for getting them. In fact, some of these boys have the notion that all the boys in residence go home every week end. This misconception is an example of the folklore and rumor that develops around correctional facilities, among new admissions. They may try to secure information about the furloughs from other boys and from the employees. But it is in the guided group interaction sessions that every boy learns how to get a furlough. He discovers that the director may decide to give him one, although this is rarely done. Usually, boys ask the members of their therapy group, or, in the lexicon of Highfields, "their meeting," for a furlough. Also, a "meeting" may decide for its own reasons that a member should get a furlough. The following excerpt from one of the guided group interaction sessions illustrates how most furloughs are requested. It serves, also, to point up the meaning that they have for some boys. Dan, the boy who asked for a furlough in this excerpt, had a difficult time adjusting to the program. He had stirred up considerable resentment by creating the impression that, as one of his fellow group members remarked, "You think you're better than we are. You act as if you're too good for Highfields." Moreover, Dan had been in residence for a long period of time without indicating that he was benefiting from his experiences. Although the group refused to grant him a furlough, the discussion highlighted Dan's problems and helped to make him aware of the nature of his interpersonal relations with his peers.

Dan said he wanted to ask for a third furlough. Charlie asked him why he wanted this furlough. In reply he said, "I feel that everything is closing in on me, as if the place is getting smaller and smaller and I don't think I can stand it anymore. It's just that I want to get away for awhile so when I come back I will feel better. Right now I am not helping myself. If I get away and come back maybe it will help me. Of course, I don't like to be locked up, I guess nobody does but it's hard on me." Chips interrupted and said, "I suppose you like X—— better?" Dan said he did. He added, "To tell you the truth I would rather do 6 months at X—— and know when I am going to get out than try and work my way out of here. You never know when you are leaving this place. Every time you turn around somebody hits you with a problem and you're stuck again. I just can't do time at Highfields." Tom interrupted and said, "I think you're crazy. You never get furloughs at X——, besides they lock you up. At least around here you have over 400 acres to run around in. I don't think you know what you're talking about." In reply, Dan said, "You're all wet, I just can't take a place like this and I have to get away for a few days." Brian said, "What do you expect to accomplish on your furlough? You already had 2, plus a week at home when you went back to court. That's 13 days altogether, everybody else gets 6 and now you are asking for more. To tell you the truth it seems to me that you don't want to help yourself. You have given up and getting this furlough won't help you a bit." Chips said he agreed with Brian. Brian continued, saying, "I think you just don't want to face your problems, you are just trying to escape them. Why don't you settle down and do something about it?" In reply, Dan said he just couldn't think straight these days. Brian remarked, "I think what you've been doing ever since you were turned down when you asked to go home is to show us your true self. When Mr. E—— said you were just putting on a show he was right. You've proved that every day at work. You just won't work. You started gambling again like mad." Joe interrupted and pointed out he felt Dan was gambling so much on purpose. He thought Dan was going to be sent back to court if he didn't start to help himself. Joe asked him if he planned to do that. Dan made no reply. Tom told him to answer. Dan replied that he was thinking, then he said, "I figure I'm not going to stay here much longer, I have only been here 3 months, one week and 6 days. I figure I'm going to stay here a few more weeks. It will be easier for me if I get a furlough." Joe commented, "The way you fool around and gamble and work, boy, I never saw such a lazy guy in my life." Brian said Joe was right. Chips agreed with him. The group was silent, then Dan turned to Charlie and asked him what he thought. Charlie replied, "No, I don't think so, Dan. I think this would be a bad time to give you a furlough. You are always getting away with murder anyway, if you get a furlough you would be getting away with it again. It's about time you faced your problems." Billy replied that he didn't know what to say. Brian pointed out that he agreed with all that had been said. He added, "There are reasons why boys get furloughs, they aren't gifts. A boy gets his first furlough to see what his problems are and he gets home on his second to see if he solved any. All you want to do is to kill some time. My advice to you is to kill time later, you don't have any time to kill now." Eddie said, "I hate to say no, Dan, but I can't see how it would help you. If I thought you were helping yourself, I would say yes but you aren't." Bill said as much as he would like to see Dan go home he would have to go along with the group. He added, "I think you ought to try and help yourself, at least act as if you are. You walk around here as if you are mad at the world and everyone in it. Do you think we are all against you?" Dan replied, "No, I don't think the group is against me, I think they are trying to help me." Bill asked, "Well, do you think there's anybody around here who you think isn't helping you?" Mr. E—— turned to Dan and asked him how he felt. Dan replied, "I think you are trying to help me, I just don't know what it is. I don't think you're keeping me here because you don't like me. I know it's for my own good but I feel I need a furlough badly. I can't see it any other way." Stanley and Chips stated that they agreed with the group because they couldn't understand how a furlough could be of any use at this point. Joe commented, "To me, Dan, I think you've given up. You don't even work good. You have to understand we can't do anything for you if you don't help yourself. We want to help you but you go around here mad and gamble, that's all I see you do is gamble. You act as if this was a gambling casino. Then you don't know how to get along with the M——'s. Like last Saturday, you could have done the floor all over again. Do you think Mr. M—— likes to get on boys when they do the cleaning? I don't like to work around here either but you got to do it. You act like you're better than we are. Hell, the judge sent you here the same as he sent me. Do you think he was punishing you by sending you here? I thought I was going to A—— for all the things I did. You could have got there too you know." Brian interrupted to point out that Dan had been at the Parental Home and also at X——. Dan nodded his head. The group remained silent for a few moments then Dan asked Paul what he thought. Paul said, "I don't know what to say, Dan. I have only been here a few days. I don't know anything about you." When Tom was asked he shook his head and said, "I don't like to say no, Dan, but what else can I say? I don't think you are helping yourself either. You aren't doing yourself any good around here. I know you can't take it here, I can't either but I got to. I like my freedom just as much as you do but you don't show nothing. You just act dumb. I just can't say anything but no." The group became silent. Dan, when asked what he thought about the group's comments, hesitated and slowly said, "I don't know, I just don't know."

It is customary for boys to regard some furloughs as opportunities to test the gains they have made. In the illustration below, Don describes in detail the experiences he had during his second furlough. When he arrived at Highfields, he felt that a grave injustice had been committed. In one of the group sessions he remarked, "I thought I was being picked on because my buddies did worse things than I and they all went home. I was mad at everybody, the judge, the cops, the probation officer, and even my mother." This seventeen-year-old boy had been involved in numerous violations of the rules of probation as well as in various thefts and assaults. Not only did he rebel against adult authority, he regarded himself as a "smart guy" and a peer-group leader in the community.

I got off the train and left Tony and "Quarters" and hopped the bus to N——. When I got to the door my mother met me and began crying. I began crying too. At first I was ashamed then I was glad even though I haven't cried in years. I guess I really wanted to cry. After I had a snack I told my mother I had to see my probation officer. I went down but he was out so I talked to another officer. He told me I didn't have to come back again and he would leave word I had reported. Then I went home and had lunch and stuck around the house with my mother until about 3:30. She was showing me the new paint job and the way the furniture was arranged. It was funny, my mother did that before but I never even noticed it. You know, I would stay out 3 or 4 days at a time. My brother would ask me how I liked the paint job and I would say "What paint job?" That's the way I was. In fact, one time my mother had an operation in the hospital, it was a small one and she was in the hospital a day and a half. I didn't discover it until several months later. When I left home she was there and when I came back a few days later she was still there. That's the way I was. I guess she figured I didn't care so she wasn't going to tell me about it. While we were talking, my mother was doing some sewing, that's the kind of work she does to support the house. Then about 3:30 I went out. My mother told me to be sure and get back in time for supper to see my brother. I went down to see the Monseigneur. He was out watching the construction of a new school. I figured he would be too busy to talk to me but he wasn't. Instead we talked about a couple hours. He reached in his drawer and pulled out two copies of my monthly reports. [Don laughed at this point and said he guessed his reports were getting around. He said his mother was pretty proud of them and reads them through and through.] He told me he was glad I was doing so well. He offered me a job on the school that they were building. That seemed so funny because he offered to give me a job working on the school that I got kicked out of. I told him I didn't want a job handed to me like that. I would rather get one of my own. Then he said he didn't think it was such a good idea for me to go back to the Catholic school. He explained even though the nuns were religious people, they were only human and I would be like a dog with a bad name. They would never forget all the things I did in school. Then he was so nice he offered to give me credit for the first 6 months of my junior year and the best thing for me to do was go to the public school, that they really didn't know me, I was only there 8 days then I came here and I almost finished my Junior year, I had 8 days to go. It seemed funny because the last time I talked to him was when I got kicked out. He wasn't going to let me have any credits for my junior year. He admitted it was a pretty rough thing to do but he said he had to do it in order to make me realize that I wasn't going to have my own way. I guess he was right after all. Now he is making up for it, he wants to help me. It makes me feel funny to have people do that especially after all the nasty things I did and all the names I called him. I even lost respect for him as a priest. Then I left him and was walking home when I decided to stop off at the candy store where we hung out. That was where my girl usually stays for awhile. I was having some coffee when who came to the door but Detective T——. He is the guy who practically arrested me. When he called me over I said to myself what have I done now. But boy was I surprised. He took me for a ride and he talked to me. He told me he was glad Highfields was helping me out and he offered to try and get my license back. What could I say? Here was a guy that I cussed out, I called him every name in the book. I even acted like a wise guy demanding calls to my lawyer and my mother. When he tried to talk to me about Highfields, it would do me some good, I told him to go f—— himself. Now he is trying to get my license back. Makes a guy feel funny, makes him wonder about people. I was glad I ran into him. When I left him I headed for home and had supper and met my brother. He was talking to me like a big brother even though I used to talk to him like that since he was smaller than I was like Clayton's brother. It was nice to listen to him. He was telling me about my mother and how much she depended on me. He explained if I ever got a bad report from Highfields it would break her up. After all she lives for us, she has been working so hard ever since my father died 11 years ago. She doesn't only sew she sells Christmas cards. She sets up a stand and sells cards to the workers at the factory. She likes to do that, she is paying off the house and in 4 years it will be all ours. You see if she doesn't work steady the bank will take the house away from her. She isn't doing it for herself, she must be doing it for us and I never appreciated it. After I talked to my brother I told my mother I was going out to see my girl. She told me not to get into any trouble and come back about midnight. I told her I would because I had promised Detective T—— I would. He told me he would tell the other cops not to bother me if they saw me on the street. That's what happened the last time I was home. I went to my girl's house and took her over to a meeting she was going to at school. You see she is a cheer leader. After I dropped her off I headed back to the store and guess who I ran into on the street? All the old crowd and they were all dressed up.

They said, "Hi, Don, are you coming along?" They asked me to go to New York with them but I told them not to talk to me, leave me alone. I didn't want to know them. [Joe wanted to know if they were the boys he had gotten into trouble with. He said they were, in fact, since that they had been in court and been put on probation. They were in trouble again and were waiting for the grand jury on Tuesday. He said,] Those guys are crazy. They will go out and get drunk on Monday night and appear in court on Tuesday morning drunk. I knew they were heading for New York because every Friday night they go there. I used to go with them all the time but I didn't even want to talk to them this time. I went up and waited for my girl at the store. About 10:30 I decided to go and get her and when I got to the place where the meeting was being held, she was coming out. I took her home. She asked me to come in and see her mother. At first I didn't want to go in because I didn't know how she would feel about me taking out her daughter. After all I had gotten into trouble and she might not like it but she took it pretty well. We sat and had some coffee then I went home. Guess it must have been about midnight. The next day my mother asked me to go down to the butcher shop with her. We went and I met the owner who used to talk to me all the time. You see I used to work there and he fired me because I used to act like a wise guy and he was afraid his customers wouldn't like that. He used to tell me I was smart but I was getting too smart for my own good. He is a pretty nice guy, he is only 26 years old. I told him I was working in the butcher shop and he had better not give me any bad meat because I could tell now. He offered me a job when I got out. He thinks the boy who is working there now is going back to college. So now I have the jobs I can pick from. You know I used to work in every store around there. It is like a small shopping center. I got fired from every one of them. I would work about 4 or 6 weeks, save my pay, not go any place and then I would quit. I lived the way all my friends acted. They all have good clothes, some of them have cars but they always have money because most of them can grub it from anybody. One guy steals, he has been living that way for years. Another guy sells a car every now and then, the others grub. The other boys in town think these guys are big shots. Then we went home and got ready to go to the football game. I went with my girl because she was the cheer leader, then I went into the stands. I ran into the father of a friend of mine. He is a guy who always liked me. He talked to me for awhile. I explained what had happened. Then his wife came over. She didn't know where I was, I guess he didn't tell her. Before I went to the game my mother had told me to stay out of trouble. There was bound to be a fight. You see this was a rivals' game. Both teams were unbeaten. We lost 25 to o and sure enough there was a fight but I stayed out of it. [Then he described how he went home after the game, got dressed, had supper, and attended a dance.] On the way to the dance I ran into 4 boys I had known. They were taking one of the girls over to baby-sit. Her family was having a big affair and all the kids were staying at the house where she was going to baby-sit. [Before they went to the dance his girl friend asked him to stop and say hello to her parents. He used to go to parties at her home and was very friendly with her father. Usually at these parties he would end up in the kitchen drinking beer with her father.] She told me to say nothing about where I had been or what I had done because it might upset them. So we went in and they offered us a drink. I had one highball. [After the drink they drove the girl to the home where she was going to baby-sit.] The boys asked me to go to New York with them. I told them, "No, I was going to take out my girl." They kept trying to talk me into going but I told them to let me out and I would walk to my girl's house. I walked a block and there she was. She asked me if I had been drinking. I explained what had happened and she said, "You go sticking around with those bums and you'll be in trouble again." I told her I wasn't doing that and I hoped that she believed me. [They then went to the dance. He said he had a very good time and then he walked his girl home. On the way home they stopped near her house.] I was trying to make out with my girl when all of a sudden a police car shot out of the street and a cop jumped out and he flashed his light on me. He said who is it and I told him it was D———. He said they thought someone was trying to steal the truck. I told him I was trying to take my girl home. About this time another police car came up and a cop jumped out and walked over and said, "Oh, D———, it's you" and I said yes it was me. He shook my hand and asked me what I was doing around here. I told him I was trying to take my girl home. They laughed and said okay and wished me good luck. That was funny because usually when the cops stopped me before I would give them a hard time. I would start screaming you can't do anything, you haven't got a search warrant, cursing them out, and they would end up dragging me in. I finally got my girl home. I guess I must've gotten home about 12:30. My mother was watching TV so we stayed up and watched the late show. The next morning, after breakfast, we went to church. I used to go to church all the time. I guess I liked to go. It must be in me.

You know I have been raised in a Catholic school. Before I used to go with all my friends. We never wore ties, we would just stand around in the back and maybe 15 or 16 of us would sit in two pews. It didn't feel like going to church at all. It was more like fooling around. All the time my mother would ask me to go with her because she used to sit up front, I didn't say anything this time. I sat up in front with her and my brother and I wore a tie. After church I went over to see my girl for awhile then came home and had lunch. About 2:30 I was going out and ask a friend of mine to drive me to Penn station. Instead I ran into a gang of old buddies. They offered to take me to New York where they were going but I told them I was coming back. They kept kidding me and said it would be better if I went with them. Then I asked them if they would take me to the station in N——. They had all sorts of reasons why they couldn't, not enough gas, not enough time, so I told them, the hell with them and went back home. My brother offered to take me in his car but I told him no. It was raining pretty hard and my mother didn't want me to go out in the rain. But I walked up with my brother to the bus. I told him to take care of my mother and let me know if anything happened. Before I left my mother explained my brother couldn't come up and see me every Sunday as he had an accident and was in the hospital for a few weeks and couldn't drive more than a few miles at a time. But he is nice enough to let my mother drive the car. I don't think she has missed more than one Sunday since I have been here. A couple weeks ago she had an accident. Some guy drove her off the road. She was pretty shaken up by this. It just makes me realize how much she cares for me. I never thought she would go out of her way, the way she does. I guess I'll have to make it up to her when I get out. When I got to Penn station I started looking for Tony. Once I walked right by him and didn't recognize him. He was wearing a coat and a hat and he seemed taller. Don't think he recognized me either because we walked right past each other without knowing it. Then we met on the train and we rode back together. I didn't mind coming back this time it was nice to have someone to talk to. I didn't want to tell you when I asked for the furlough I'd promise to do certain things. I didn't know if I could do them but in my mind I promised myself and I think I had a pretty successful furlough. I feel a lot closer to my family and I realize there were a lot of people who were going to help me who didn't have to help. Of course, there are always some people who don't like you like some of our neighbors but like I told my mother they weren't good friends. My mother is funny she always thinks there is a lot of good in everyone.

Another form of community contact made by the boys is through monthly reports of their adjustment which are sent to the judge and to the probation officers. These evaluations are prepared in part by the boy himself as well as by his group. After the reports are completed, they are discussed by the group. In this way everyone involved in a case is kept informed periodically of the progress of each boy during his career at Highfields. Also, in many instances, these reports give the boys an opportunity to take stock of themselves—in a sense, to declare a moratorium on their activities—in order to "see what's been happening to me so far."

III

The Highfields Resident

IN ORDER TO FURTHER OUR UNDERSTANDING OF THE SOCIAL ORGANIZA-
tion of Highfields, it is necessary to clarify the function and the
social roles of the boys and the staff who live and work there.

THE BOYS

The problem of examining the role of the boys is a complex
one, for it is possible to do so from a variety of viewpoints. Even
from the vantage point of the staff there is no clear-cut conception of the role the boys ought to play at Highfields. In a conventional correctional facility, it is possible for the adminstration
to categorize the inmates for specific purposes, such as custody
and/or treatment. In such facilities, some inmates are security
risks and others are not; some inmates are improvable offenders
while others are non improvable; or, they are regarded in terms
of the degree of their involvement in crime—as professional rack-
eteers, gangsters, habitual petty thieves, occasional offenders. Then
too, they may be viewed from a psychiatric point of view and
categorized in terms of their psychopathological difficulties. However, at Highfields, there is no formal categorization of the boys.
There are no trusties or honor boys. In fact, there is no merit
system or any other device which normally differentiates inmates.

However, occasionally, in discussing the boys, a member of the
staff will classify some of them according to the kinds of experiences he has had with them up to that time. He may feel that
some boys are "wise guys," that others are mixed-up boys, and
that still others are babies. At the same time, he may categorize

them as "good boys," boys who are "trying to learn something," boys who are "ready to go home," and still others as boys who "need a lot of help." From the point of view of the boys themselves, it is difficult to determine subjectively what it means to be at Highfields. Sometimes they laughingly refer to themselves as "bad boys." A boy will point out somewhat facetiously, "I'm a J.D." A shrewd, sophisticated, urbanized boy may regard himself as a very important person with confidence and self-assurance and ability to cope with any situation in a self-satisfying way. Still others regard themselves as bewildered and confused, living in a world of anxiety, hoping, believing blindly that out of this chaos there will emerge a world of order and security for them; and a few see themselves as hopelessly inadequate, helpless in a world which is organized against them and whose ultimate goal is to destroy them.

Perhaps the most conspicuous way the boys relate with one another is in terms of the social roles they play. Some of these roles are brought with them from the community, while others are created at Highfields. The kind of role which a boy plays is not fixed, nor does he play, necessarily, a single role at any one point in his career. Since there is no formal orientation of boys by the staff, they are assigned roles when they arrive by the other boys in residence, or they assume social roles of their own choosing. Regardless of the kind of role a boy plans to assign to himself at Highfields, on the day he arrives he is regarded as a "new boy." The kinds of expectations which have been assigned to this role as a result of experience through the years must be fulfilled, or else conflict develops. The only other fixed role at Highfields is that of an "old boy." There are also certain expectations which have developed around this role. One of these is that an "old boy" be in residence longer than most of the other boys. Another, which is not always fulfilled is, as one boy pointed out, "You act in a way which shows us that you are getting ready to go home." Sometimes a boy who has been in residence for quite a while is admonished by his group because "You are not acting like an old boy. You haven't shown that you are learning anything at Highfields." Between these two roles there is a broad range of social roles which boys play in their relationships with each other, such as "Duke," "punk," "hipster," "wise guy," "regular guy," "ball buster," "agitator," "mystery man," and a host of others. Some of these roles are highly esteemed, while others are not. However, it is entirely possible for a boy to play a variety of roles during his career. In looking back over his experiences at Highfields, one boy was able to perceive the roles which he played, and wrote in the following manner:

What I think I done in the last three months and three weeks at Highfields. I could remember the first day I came. I got out of the car and looked around. The place looked so strange to me at first, Then I went inside looked around again, It was about dinner time, so I put my clothes down and went in to eat. The first boys I met were John & Walter, I took them as reguler guys, I ate my dinner then Pop showed me where I was to sleep, It was a big room I slept on a top bunk. Then I changed my clothes and Pop put me to work. About five o'clock the rest of the boys came home. Some of the boys I didn't like at first I didn't know them but the way they looked at me. That night I had a good sleep, At first I didn't like to go to the meetings. I didn't go for days at a time I used to go to sleep and other times I fooled around the house. The first few weeks I didn't like it here The guys used to call me new boy get this and that, At first I stood there like a dope and took it in. I had a couple of fights after work but it didn't help, I just didn't know what to do at first and didn't care, but as the weeks went on, I started to defend myself and call them back names, got in to some more fights, even if I got beat, I still fought back, After about a month and a half I was one of the boys, then they started calling me Duke it went to my head, and I started turning a wise guy, but after a certain party left I became a regular guy.

Another way to determine differences between the boys is to present a brief statistical view of some of their social characteristics.

The various county judges who select boys for residence at Highfields are guided by a set of formal criteria. While these criteria provide some indication of the type of offenders involved, they do not shed light on other factors which distinguish these boys and the range of social differences between them.

The data which are presented for analysis below were not selected because they provide an exhaustive or a complete picture
of the probationers at Highfields. Rather, they are intended to
provide a general overview of some of the social factors which
distinguish the boys from each other.

Moreover, no attempt was made to subject this material to
detailed statistical analysis. Our aim, in this section, is merely
to present a brief, general picture of the boys and to indicate
gross differences between them.[4]

When Highfields was initiated, four of the most populous
counties in the state agreed to start the program by sending boys
to the project. Throughout its brief history, they have supplied
the bulk of the population. As Chart 1 indicates, more then four
fifths of all the boys were admitted from Essex, Bergen, Hudson,
and Union Counties. These counties, which are located in the
northern part of the state, are each dominated by a large industrialized community. Passaic County, which is also highly urbanized, began sending boys about three years after the project got
under way. The remaining counties are dominated largely by
semirural, small industrialized, or resort and recreational centers.[5]

Chart 1 describes also the range of offenses that have been committed by the 317 probationers who were admitted for residence.
Most of these boys were involved in more than a single offense
at the time they were apprehended. For purposes of this chart,
we have selected in each case the most serious offense. The largest
single category is offenses against property, which includes almost
two thirds of all offenses. The second largest category was other
offenses, which includes about one fifth of all the cases. Within
this group of offenses is incorrigibility, which is a catch-all offense
and includes violation of the rules of probation, "problem boys,"
traffic violations, drinking, running away from home, and destruction of property. The offenses against other persons includes, for

---

[4] The data which are analyzed below were secured from admission cards collected during the first five years of the operation of Highfields, namely from
July 1, 1950, until June 30, 1955. It should be noted that the first boy admitted to Highfields arrived during the second week of July, 1950.
[5] There are 21 counties in New Jersey; 14, or two thirds, of all the counties
in the state had utilized the facilities at Highfields by June 30, 1955.

CHART 1
Social Characteristics of 317 Admissions
(numbers indicate percentages)

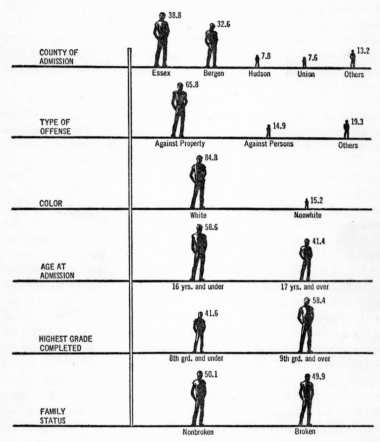

the most part, boys who were charged with statutory rape. A few cases involved carnal abuse and indecent exposure. In no instance was an active homosexual included in this category.

The third category in this chart shows that less than one sixth of all admissions were Negroes. Spread over a five-year period, this means that less than ten Negro boys were admitted each year during the past five years. On one occasion, however, there were more Negro boys in residence than white boys. It may be possible to account for the relatively small proportion of Negroes at Highfields as compared with the proportion of Negroes in conventional correctional facilities in terms of the criteria for admission. To be admitted, boys must be at least sixteen years of age and without any previous institutionalization in a state correctional facility. By and large, urban Negro males tend to be involved in official delinquencies at an earlier age than urban white males. The chances are, then, that Negro boys will have been committed to the state training school in greater proportion than white boys before reaching their sixteenth birthday. As a result, the number of sixteen to eighteen-year-old Negro boys who appear before a juvenile court judge for disposition to Highfields is reduced considerably.

Although the age limits for admission to the project are sixteen and seventeen years, we have admitted boys who are beyond this age range. If a fifteen-year-old boy fulfills the other qualifying criteria, he is eligible for admission if he will attain his sixteenth birthday during his residence at Highfields. Also, an eighteen-year-old boy will be admitted, provided he committed his offense prior to his eighteenth birthday. This accounts for the presence of the fifteen and eighteen-year-old boys in Chart 1. It is interesting to note that more than half of the boys were sixteen years old or less at the time of their admission.

Although there is no indication, in the criteria which guide judges in the selection of probationers for Highfields, that a certain level of educational attainment is necessary, more than half of the boys completed a portion of their high-school training. However, almost none of these boys were attending school at the time of their admission to Highfields. In fact, the overwhelming majority of them had been expelled or had been asked to leave school upon reaching their sixteenth birthday. Furthermore, only a handful of them expressed interest in returning to school after leaving Highfields.

The literature in this field attributes an important role to the

character of the family relationships in the etiology of delinquency. Some studies have indicated that the broken home factor
is not crucial in this respect.[6] This chart reveals that, insofar as
Highfields boys are concerned, the external structure of the family relationship was not a factor in selection for admission. Half
the boys came from broken homes, and the other half from homes
which were outwardly intact.

THE STAFF

The Highfields residents includes the employees as well as the
boys, for the director, the cottage supervisors, and the intern live
in the same dwelling. The secretary and the work supervisor
live off the property.

In most correctional facilities, especially where custody is paramount, the ratio of inmates to staff tends to be low, whereas in
institutions for children the ratio tends to be higher. For example, in 1953, it was estimated that there was one full-time
employee (professional, administrative, and maintenance) for
every 2.4 children resident in public state training schools in
the United States.[7] At Highfields a minimal staff was organized,
so that over the years the ratio of staff to boys has been about
one employee for every 3.3 boys. One of the reasons for this
ratio is that there is no need to maintain a custodial force or an
extensive clerical staff.

Perhaps the most obvious function of the staff as a whole,
which consists of six employees, is to work toward the maintenance of routine services that fulfill the minimal conditions of
living. Also, since the staff is relatively small in size, it is necessary
and it is expected that each employee play a variety of roles.
Occasionally this situation leads to a discrepancy between the
official definition of each position and the individual's actual
performance of his role. However, there is present in each em-

---

[6] C. Shaw and H. D. McKay, *Social Factors in Juvenile Delinquency.* U. S.
Gov't. Printing Office: Washington, D. C., 1951, Chapter IX, pp. 261–284.
[7] "Some Facts About Public State Training Schools For Juvenile Delinquents,"
Children's Bureau Statistical Series No. 33, 1956, p. 19.

ployee's conception of his role an overriding view which sets the pattern for satisfying the formal requirements of the job as well as the informal demands of their daily work, and that is "to help the boys." Since the members of the staff work closely with the boys, life at Highfields can become very intense and occasionally takes on the character of the relationships which are found in large households. It should be noted, though, that no formal attempt is made to structure the interpersonal relationships between the staff and the boys in terms of a family situation. As much as a boy or an employee may desire to establish familial bonds with each other, the reality of "being away from home" is continually being thrust upon each boy as the pressures mount for him and especially upon an employee, when a conflict situation arises where his authority is seriously challenged. Moreover, since each employee develops his own conception of what actions on his part constitute "help," oftentimes a confusing situation arises, especially from the point of view of the boys who may be trapped between conflicting definitions. Disagreements and misunderstandings may result from the fact that two employees may establish social bonds with one boy which are at variance with each other. These conflict situations provide some of the raw day-to-day experiences which are discussed in the guided group interaction sessions. In many respects the stability of relationships between the boys and the staff are supported in and occasionally created out of these group discussions.

THE DIRECTOR

As formally constituted, the director at Highfields has a dual role—namely, therapist and administrator. He is charged with the overall responsibility of conducting the program, including the supervision of the other five employees. As therapist, he conducts the guided group interaction sessions in the evening, and as administrator, he performs a variety of functions. He conducts correspondence, prepares monthly and annual reports, sets up the annual budget in addition to other kinds of financial reports; in a sense, he acts as business manager. A second aspect of his job as administrator requires that he make public appearances from time to time when he discusses the Highfields program with civic and professional organizations as well as with employees at institutions which are conducting in-service training programs. Of course, he meets with groups of visitors who wish to acquaint themselves with the program. Around the house, in the absence of the cottage supervisors, the director assumes their duties, including getting the boys up and off to work in the morning and supervising them after their return from work in the early evening. He acts in this capacity for a period of four days every ten days. Since the boys work at a nearby state hospital, lunches must be brought to them each day. The director performs this assignment. Also, he takes boys to the hospital for first aid care and for inoculations and medical examinations. From time to time boys are granted furloughs. Since there is no public transportation in the vicinity, the director transports the boys to and from the railroad station, which is located about ten miles from the house. These trips occur on Friday morning and Sunday evening.

Still another phase of the director's work as administrator requires that he maintain continuous contact with the juvenile courts and probation departments that send boys to Highfields. It is imperative that the judges and their probation officers be informed about the adjustment of the boys from their counties as well as about any developments at Highfields. It is almost axiomatic that a close and understanding relationship between Highfields and the county officials is one of the cornerstones of the program. By sharing knowledge which is gained about each boy, adequate decisions can be made regarding his future disposition. For this reason, the director visits the various courts and probation offices from time to time and, in turn, receives periodic visits from judges and probation officers.

A major aspect of the work of the director is his role as therapist. As such, he conducts guided group interaction sessions five evenings every week. On these evenings, he meets with two groups of boys for an hour and a half each, usually from 7:00 P.M. to 10:00 P.M.

There are other assorted jobs which any director of a correctional facility is called upon to perform also, such as greeting official visitors, meeting with tradesmen, attending meetings in the central office, inspecting the building, supervising other employees, and making numerous decisions.[8] A glance at the work load, Tables 1 through 5, will provide a general picture of the work of the director as well as that of the other employees.

WORKLOAD DATA

TABLE 1

Boys' Work

Details		Period of Work	Supervising Employee
At NJNPI			
Garbage	3 boys	Daily (incl. Sat.)	Institute driver
Butcher shop	1 boy	Daily	Institute butcher
Farm	Remaining boys	Daily	Work supervisor
At HIGHFIELDS			
K.P.	1 boy	Daily	Asst. cottage supr.
Housecleaning	All boys	Sat. morn.	Cottage supervisor and director

---

[8] It is difficult within the scope of this report to present a detailed and critical analysis of each of the roles which the director plays in his relations with different groups of people such as other public officials, the employees, and the boys. The same situation exists, of course with regard to the other employees whose work is discussed below. A major area of concern here would be the relationship between the director and the boys, which presents complex problems. For example, the question is often raised about the relationship between the role of the director as therapist versus his role as an authority. Whether or not this is a real dilemma or one which has been created by theoreticians is a moot point. We do not propose to deal with it here.

TABLE 2

Contacts with Community

Specific Task	Time Period	Supervising Employee
All Boys		
Transp. to church	Sun. morns.	Sociological intern or director
Transp. to movies	Sat. eves.	Sociological intern & supt. of boys
Transp. to town for personal shopping, haircuts, etc.	Sat. afts.	Sociological intern or director
Transp. to and from train on furloughs	Fri. morns. & Sun. eves.	Sociological intern or director

TABLE 3

Guided Group Interaction

Specific Task	Time Period	Supervising Employee
Guided group interaction sessions	Every eve. except Thurs., and Sat. from 7:00 P.M.–10:00 P.M.	Director
Number of sessions conducted per group each year	90	Director
Number of groups each year	10	Director

TABLE 4

Public Relations

Specific Tasks	Time Period	Supervising Employee
Correspondence (all reports, typing & dictation)	Daily	Sr. clerk-steno.
Filing	Daily	Sr. clerk-steno.
Annual reports	Yearly	Director & sr. clerk-steno.
Research reports	Occasionally	Director & sr. clerk-steno.
Public appearances	Occasionally	Director
Visits to juvenile courts & prob. depts.	Bimonthly	Director
Meeting visitors	Occasionally	Director

TABLE 5

Maintenance

Specific Tasks	Time Period	Supervising Employee
Maint. of all equip., including household, electrical, plumbing, and heating, carpentry, masonry	Daily	Cottage supervisor
Grounds & landscaping	Daily	Cottage supervisor
Cooking	Daily	Ass't cottage supr., intern, & director
Supervision of boys around house	Daily	Cottage supervisor, intern, & director
Bed check	Daily	Director & intern
Supervision after hours	Daily	Director & intern

WORK SUPERVISOR

When the boys are working away from the house at a nearby state hospital, as they do each weekday, they are under the direct supervision of the work supervisor. This position, which requires a bachelor's degree and some experience in working with delinquent boys, involves two main tasks: supervising the boys at work at the hospital, and taking them to town on Saturday evenings. At work, he not only manages the boys but is responsible also for their production. Each weekday, he transports the boys to the hospital, which is located about five miles from Highfields. There he assigns the boys to several jobs under the supervision of hospital personnel. He himself undertakes the management of the largest group of boys—namely, the farm detail—after the head farmer has set up the day's work. The remaining boys, usually four or five, are assigned to hospital employees in the butcher shop and on the garbage detail. In the evening, the work supervisor returns all the boys to Highfields. In addition, on Saturday evenings, he shares the responsibility with the intern of taking the boys to town to attend the movies, to purchase refreshments, and to make phone calls.

Although he is in constant contact with the boys during the day, his role in relation to them is analogous to that of foreman in a factory. He does not manage the boys in the same sense that a guard or correction officer manages a group of inmates in a custodial institution. As Cressy has pointed out, "Most guards have nothing to do but guard, they do not use inmates productively any more than they, in their role as guards are used productively by prison managers. They manage and are managed in organizations where management is an end, not a means." [9] The work supervisor is primarily responsible for production, although he has the secondary task of coping with the personal and group problems of the boys as they are expressed in the work situation.

[9] Donald R. Cressy, "Social Organization of Correctional Institutions." Department of Sociology, University of California, Los Angeles, unpublished paper.

For the most part, the boys see him as one boy remarked: "H——
is like a boss or a foreman, just like a boss on the job at home."
As is the case with the secretary, he does not reside at the house;
consequently, unlike the cottage supervisor, he has only restricted
opportunities for interacting with the boys on a more informal
basis than he does at work.

COTTAGE SUPERVISORS

It is becoming increasingly evident that lower echelon personnel in a correctional administrative hierarchy play a vital role in
determining the impact of the institutional program upon the
inmates. In a sense, the manner in which these employees—the
guards or correctional officers in prisons and reformatories, and
cottage parents and officers in training schools—relate with the
inmates in the daily process of social interaction "determines in
the long run not only the care and treatment policy of the institution but that of the larger society as well." [10] These employees stand as surrogates of society and bring to bear the power of
the state and the pressures of the institutional policies and programs on the inmates, in a very concrete and detailed manner. It
is almost commonplace today, in the field of correction, to point
to the necessity for radically modifying the role of these employees
in order to increase the effectiveness of treatment programs and
even of custody.[11]

At Highfields, the cottage supervisors play important roles in
the lives of each boy, if only because they are in a position to
interact with the boys more frequently than any of the other employees. These supervisors are a married couple with no previous
training or experience in correctional work. However, whether

---

[10] Lloyd W. McCorkle and R. Korn, "Resocialization Within Walls," *Annals*,
Vol. 293, May 1954, p. 93.
[11] An attempt to achieve this aim by making the cottages in a training school
for boys and girls the center of the treatment program was largely unsuccessful
because of the failure of the cottage parents to accept the program. See S.R.
Slavson, *Re-educating the Delinquent Through Group and Community Participation*. New York: Harpers, 1954, pp. 251.

it is due to their lack of formal training, the flexible nature of their jobs, or their interest in their work, they are able to relate with the boys in a spontaneous, noninstitutional way. As a result, the boys are able to interact with them as adults they may have met in the past, rather than as objects who fill a prescribed role. In effect, they are interacting with Mr. and Mrs. M—— and not with the cottage supervisors. This informal relationship assists in gaining knowledge about and understanding of each boy's attitude toward adults rather than attitudes toward specific institutional roles. Moreover, it places the boys in a position to meet with them in a fairly nonthreatening setting.[12]

The cottage supervisors have the formal responsibility of overall supervision of the boys when they are at home. Over and above this assignment, the male supervisor performs other duties which involve the maintenance and upkeep of the equipment and the fixtures in the building, as well as the maintenance of the grounds in the area immediately surrounding the house. Also, when a boy is "working in the pit" because of some infraction, he is directly supervised by this employee. On Saturday mornings when the boys clean the house, he shares with his wife the job of supervising the boys. Sometimes, in the evenings and on Sundays when there is no work to be done, he will circulate throughout the house conversing with various boys.

The assistant cottage supervisor serves mainly as the cook and a sort of housemother. She prepares all the meals with the help of one boy who acts as K.P. Also, she devotes a considerable portion of her time to talking to the boys. Many boys will consult her regarding her opinion of the kind of adjustment they are making. Many times a boy will go into the kitchen merely to talk to her about "his problems," largely because a boy feels that it is easier to talk to her than to any other employee.

---

[12] In this regard, Reckless has indicated that "the non-professional personnel more than the professional personnel come closest to the inmates, help the most, understand them the best and generally exert the greatest impact on them . . . ," quoted in an unpublished paper by Walter C. Reckless, "The Impact of Correctional Programs on Inmates." School of Social Service Administration, Ohio State University.

SOCIOLOGICAL INTERN

Originally, the internship position at Highfields was established by a grant from the Vincent Astor Foundation because the trustees in the Foundation recognized the need of providing assistance in the training of qualified persons in this field. The interns were graduate students in sociology who remained in residence for a period of one year. After experimenting with this program for several years, the State of New Jersey undertook to establish the internship as a permanent part of the Highfields program with a twofold aim: (1) to provide training in the techniques of guided group interaction, and (2) to provide an opportunity to gain intimate knowledge of delinquent boys through close contact with them.

The duties of the intern are generalized. Initially he assists the superintendent in the performance of various tasks such as cooking, transporting boys to various places, and putting the boys to bed. Also, he attends the group sessions, and after observing them for a period of time he is given leadership of one of the two therapy groups. In this way he receives firsthand knowledge and experience in the techniques of conducting a therapy group.

In many ways the intern is in a peculiar position in his relationship with the boys. The kind of relationships which he develops with the boys depends upon many factors. In time, he is recognized as a person in a position of authority. However, occasionally the boys will become confused about the limits of his authority. This confusion develops, in part, because of his role as group leader. Since the director is the "official authority" and is also acting in the capacity of group leader, the boys may wonder whether the intern, too, is an "official authority." As a result, conflicting situations develop which indicate that the boys are testing the limits of his authority. However, over a period of time, as his role becomes defined more clearly, his decisions tend to become accepted more readily by the boys.

SECRETARY

Of all the employees at Highfields, the secretary plays the most formal role. This is largely the result of the fact that there is a minimum of interaction between her and the boys. Because her work is restricted to the office during her work week, her only contacts with the boys are on the days they arrive and when they happen to be on K.P. Since her duties are confined to the office routine, there is little opportunity for defining her role in any other but in a formal sense.

IV

The Highfields Structure

THE TOTAL PROGRAM OF A MODERN AMERICAN CORRECTIONAL FACILity operates within the framework of a relatively large, complex, social organization. The large numbers and various types of inmates who inhabit them, the bureaucratic structure that regulates the system of relationships between the custodial, treatment, and clerical members of the staff, the numerous buildings and the maze of offices, as well as the involved set of rules and regulations that govern the conduct of the inmates in their relationships with the staff and with each other are characteristic features of such institutions. Each facility, then, has a formal organization which follows a master plan. For example, a prison has been defined as "a physical structure in a geographical location where a number of people living together under highly specialized conditions utilize the resources and adjust to the alternatives presented to them by a unique kind of social environment. The formal administrative structure of the prison may be comprehended in a brief glance at its table of organization. This table reveals a series of bureaucratically arranged positions with the Warden at the top and the formal flow of power downward from his position." [13]

In contrast with this involved bureaucratic structure that may be found in a conventional correctional facility, the Highfields social structure is simple in design. In a sense, the entire facility

---

[13] Lloyd W. McCorkle and Richard Korn, "Resocialization Within Walls," *Annals*, Vol. 293, May 1954, p. 88. See also, American Prison Association, *A Manual of Correctional Standards*, 1954, pp. 49–51, for a thoroughly rationalized conception of the administrative structure of a prison.

represents a single, almost natural unit. Everyone with the exception of two employees resides in one relatively small building. There is an absence of formal rules to regulate the interaction between the various people who live and work at the house. Boys come and go at the rate of about five each month, so that at the end of a period of one year sixty boys will have been exposed to the program. We have then, both a changing and a constant social system at Highfields. An analysis of the major aspects of this system will enhance an understanding of the nature of the program and the social situation in which it operates.

THE PHYSICAL STRUCTURE

Highfields is located in the Sourland Mountains of Central New Jersey. The house is situated in a densely wooded area, about three miles from Hopewell, a suburban community, and approximately fifteen miles from the state capital, which is the nearest metropolitan center. The grounds, which comprise almost four hundred acres, are uncultivated except for the area immediately adjoining the house. This area is landscaped simply and provides sufficient space for a driveway, a back yard and a small lawn which is dotted with large boulders. The back yard serves as a basketball court, the only recreation area on the property. While there are three large open fields about a half mile from the house, they are seldom used for recreational purposes by the boys. Periodically, a group of boys will organize themselves into teams and play touch tackle or baseball, depending upon the season of the year, on one of these fields. However, this interest is hardly ever sustained. The one sport which is played the year round is basketball, largely because of the easy access to the court but, in part, due to the fact that this activity does not require much equipment, players, or formal organization.

The only house on the property serves as a dwelling place for the boys as well as for the director and his family, the intern, and the cottage parents. To all intents and purposes, the house is divided into two parts, for there are two stairways leading to the upstairs quarters on each side of the house. The employees reside

upstairs on one side of the house, while the boys occupy two
rooms upstairs on the other side. In addition to the two rooms
which have been set aside as dormitories for the boys, the first
floor contains the director's office, the dining room, the pantry,
the kitchen, the intern's room, and a bathroom. All told, there
are fourteen rooms in the house. Moreover, in the basement there
are additional rooms: a furnace room, two storerooms, and a
small workshop for the cottage supervisor. Also, there is a three
car garage on the side of the house underneath two of the boys'
rooms.

This description indicates the severe limitations which the
physical structure of the house provides, especially in view of the
fact that there is no room set aside for indoor activities. During
the spring, summer, and early fall months, many of the boys'
activities are carried on outside the house. They take walks
through the woods and play softball and a few other outdoor
games. Since there is no organized recreation program, the choice
of activities lies with the boys themselves. Outdoor activities are
severely restricted during the winter months. During this period,
the boys engage in other types of recreation, i.e., card playing,
chess, checkers, assorted group games such as tag, "jail," pillow
fights, dancing, wrestling, weight lifting, and boxing. Each of the
boys' rooms has individual lockers or closets, a table, and chairs,
so that much of the interaction between the boys takes place during cold and rainy days in these quarters.

The boys frequently use each others' rooms as places for gathering, particularly immediately before and after meal times and
during week ends. However, after breakfast and before supper, many boys congregate in the kitchen where they "social-
ize" with the cook and the cottage supervisor and sometimes assist the cook in preparing one or two items of food. Also, the
kitchen is used as a thoroughfare, so that there is a great deal
of movement in and around it. The dining room is used infrequently and then only for an occasional card game or for letter-
writing purposes. Boys who engage in weight lifting perform
their exercises in the garage. The only other gathering place is
the patio that runs the full length of the back of the house. It

is used only during warm and clear days, sometimes for sunbathing, and other times just for browsing, card playing, and rough, aggressive interplay. Of course, the office is used as a meeting place where the guided group interaction sessions are held in the evening.

Other than the kitchen, there is no real social center in the house. Usually, in the evening, after returning from work and showering, some of the boys head directly for the kitchen. Sometimes they merely stand around and watch the cook preparing supper. Occasionally, they will converse with her, other times they will assist her. It is interesting to note that for shy, immature, new boys, the kitchen provides "someplace to go." In a sense, this is a way of escaping and avoiding other boys. Gradually, however, over a period of several days, these new boys move out from the kitchen into the boys' rooms. Of course, some boys congregate in the kitchen because they feel they will be able to impress the cook and her husband, the cottage supervisor, with their "sincerity and goodness." Largely because this kind of behavior is frowned upon by the other boys, who define this activity as "brown-nosing," and in part because the cottage parents discourage boys from becoming "pets," few boys persist in this kind of behavior. Perhaps the real significance of socializing in the kitchen for boys who have been in residence for a fairly long period of time, is an opportunity to discuss their problems informally with the employees. It may be that a boy is having difficulting relating with one or both of the cottage parents. Sometimes they resent their authority or rebel against their demands and engage in loud and prolonged arguments during periods when they work around the house. In these instances the therapy group may encourage a boy to "go in the kitchen and talk things over with Mrs. M—— so you can straighten things out." Also, there are times when a boy's attitude toward authority is clearly revealed in his attitude toward the kitchen. For example, if a boy deliberately and assiduously avoids hanging around the kitchen, walks through the kitchen only when necessary, and avoids greeting the cook, invariably someone, including the cook herself, will question the boy regarding this behavior. She will want to know why he refuses to stay in the kitchen, or why he refuses to greet her and talk with her. Although some to the boys reject these invitations, most of them gradually accept, particularly when they observe other boys engaging in easy conversation with the cook and anyone else there. Very often it is in the kitchen that the boys receive their initial encouragement to take advantage of the guided group interaction sessions, either from the cook directly or from listening to a small group of boys discuss with the cook the incidents and problems which they are planning to bring up in the meetings. In the sense then, the kitchen tends to take on a very special significance for numerous boys.

Other areas which are used even more frequently by the boys are the rooms in which they sleep. However, no single room is regarded as a social center by all the boys. From time to time, one of the rooms becomes a "local hangout." This means that most of the boys will congregate in that room when they are home, either to gamble, argue, listen to the radio, conduct bull sessions, play games, wrestle, or, many times, to discuss the problems of a particular boy or group. This "hangout," however, shifts from room to room and from group to group. The movement of the social center from one area to another depends on a variety of factors. A very popular boy will attract a host of other boys to his room, particularly if there is a radio in it. For example, in discussing this particular problem one boy said, "I live upstairs but I hang out in the big room downstairs because most of the boys are in there, but I think that everybody is now going upstairs in the small room but I don't know why. I guess if I want to find something to do from now on I will have to stay upstairs." Another boy replied, "Yeah, everybody is coming upstairs but that's mostly because the radio was moved up there. Besides, I think that most of the guys who come up there are interested in cars anyway. We're always talking about cars. We've already finished cars that we haven't even started building." Sometimes the social center moves to a room which is least visible to employees, either because the boys feel that it is easier to gamble there without getting caught or because they want to engage in group singing or another group activity. Of course, when there is a clique of boys, living in one room, who dominate the activities around the house, most of the other boys will congregate in that room. Sometimes the boys who sleep in one room, usually one of the smaller rooms, will form a cohesive minority group to make up their rules regarding who is to be permitted the use of their room. Occasionally, they will go so far as to put signs on the door notifying nonmembers to keep out. At other times, although infrequently, boys will divide themselves into two groups for types of "raiding," such as pillow fights—the boys who sleep upstairs versus the boys who sleep downstairs.

An area which is especially significant in the lives of the boys is the garage. It is used for parking cars and as a place where boys engage in assorted activities. Through the years, there has developed an expression regarding the garage which has a special meaning and which every boy learns, namely, "let's go to the garage." To the boys, this is an invitation to fight another boy, although actually very few fights are held there. The expression is used as a threat—sometimes in jest, sometimes seriously—whenever two boys feel they cannot settle their differences verbally or by avoiding each other.

It can be seen then, that the physical construction of the house plays an important role in circumscribing the kinds of activities in which the boys will engage and the areas in which they will be carried on, as well as helping to define the nature of the social relations which exist between the staff and the boys as well as between the boys themselves. The absence of the usual trappings which are found in conventional institutions encourages the establishment of an informal atmosphere. There are no signs or bulletin boards anywhere in the house. The only note of formality in the house is the K.P. List which can be found posted on one side of the refrigerator in the kitchen. The rooms are identified in part by the use to which they are put and in part by their location. For example, boys' rooms are identified as the big room downstairs, the little room downstairs, the big room upstairs and the little room upstairs. In this way we have tried to minimize the "institutionalization" of Highfields.

RULES AND REGULATIONS

Ordinarily, the range of choices that are available to inmates in correctional institutions are severely limited by a prescribed set of rules and regulations. The maintenance of order and discipline among the inmates is oftentimes the principle which sets the limits of inmate conduct. With some qualifications, inmates are neither expected nor permitted to make decisions for themselves. Their daily lives are planned and directed for them. At Highfields, however, there is a minimum of formal rules which apply to the boys, and most of them were established to make it possible to maintain the routine, day-to-day, existence of about thirty people who live together in one house. Also, they were designed to provide the boys with opportunities to make their own decisions and to act out their own definitions within a broad range of alternatives.

There are two kinds of rules at Highfields: general or formal rules, of which there are only two; and informal rules, which are innumerable. The two fixed rules are (1) the boys are not permitted to leave the property without being accompanied by an adult, and (2) the boys are not permitted to engage in conversation with the female patients at the state hospital where they work. The character of the informal rules varies from time to time and from group to group. It may be that one of the employees decides to put a rule into effect in order to make his own work more efficient. If he feels that it is of sufficient importance to require the approval of the director, he will discuss it with him. Ordinarily, however, this is not necessary. For example, on Thursday evenings in recent years, five boys are permitted to go to town to make purchases in the candy store. The employee who is responsible for this task decided to appoint one boy as secretary. It is his responsibility to take orders from the other boys in the house and select four boys to accompany him and the employee. This matter came to the attention of the director informally. Various techniques were worked out by these secretaries to carry out this much sought-after assignment. Of course, this role of the secretary is carefully supervised in order to insure that every boy gets his turn. A technique devised by one of the secretaries was to pick boys alphabetically. Another secretary chose the method of selecting one boy from each room, a third secretary decided to institute a rule that a boy had to be a resident at Highfields for at least three weeks before he could take his turn. Because there is a change of secretaries every eight to ten weeks, the rules for selecting boys to go to town also change. The rules, then, are flexible in their application from boy to boy and from time to time.

Since there is a minimum of ordering and forbidding, the rules take on assorted meanings, depending upon how each boy perceives them. For example, in describing his attitude toward one of the fixed rules, one boy stated, "I figured it was all right to leave the property, if you did it once. That way I could say it was an accident and, you know, anybody can have an accident." Another boy declared, "I'd never leave the property, I wouldn't take the chance." Still another boy expressed a notion that is common among Highfields boys when he remarked, "I know it's wrong to walk off the property, you told me about it when I first came here, but so long as I thought you didn't know about it, I was going to do it whenever I felt like doing it. But now that I discovered you knew about it all the time, I don't think I'll be going off again." Occasionally, a new boy will rationalize his behavior in this way: "I didn't intend to go off the property, three of us decided to go for a walk in the woods and before we knew it we were on the road somewhere. We just got lost you might say." Since the boundaries of the property are not clearly marked, it is possible to go beyond them without realizing it. One boy who had walked off the property explained this act in these terms: "All I did was to put one foot on the road past the gate just to see what it was like to smell free air. There aren't any locks or guards or bars on the windows at Highfields. I know that. But there are bars in my mind. I just had to break out once, just once. It sure smelled good, believe me."

Because the rules are forever being challenged by the boys, there is a constant conflict, particularly during the early stages of a boy's career at Highfields. The motivation to challenge the rules involves, at times, a deliberate, conscious plan to test the limits of Highfields. At other times, it is unconscious, and a boy is surprised to learn the meaning of this conduct when it is discussed in the guided group interaction sessions. Of course, many boys get caught up in a small peer group's decision to violate the rules, without fully realizing what is happening to them. Other boys occasionally blunder into defecting because they were too bewildered or too upset to understand the rules when they were explained on the day they arrived.

The consequences for violating the rules are not prescribed in the sense that violation of a particular rule involves a particular set of consequences. Violations are interpreted and consequences are applied in terms of the meaning of the act to the boy or group of boys involved. Also, defections are interpreted in terms of their effect on other boys in the house and their feelings about it. Of course, much is dependent also upon the particular employee who may be involved in the situation, and his feelings at the moment play an important part in determining what will happen to a boy who violates a rule. To many boys it seems to be an arbitrary and bewildering state of affairs. This is particularly true in the case of boys who have had previous institutionalization, either in an orphanage, private school, or a detention facility. On one occasion a boy who had considerable institutional experience prior to his experience at Highfields stated his case in regard to the rules in this way, "It would be a lot easier for me if you could give me a list of the rules around here so that I would know what I was suppose to do. Then I would never get in trouble because I would know what not to do. This way, Mr. M—— makes up his rules whenever he feels like it. Then, Mrs. M—— makes up different rules. Then sometimes, Mr. F—— decides to make up another rule. I don't know what to do. Every time I turn around I find myself getting into trouble. Why doesn't somebody give me a list of rules? I don't know whether I'm coming or going. At J——, everybody had a set of rules. It didn't take long to find out what they were. I wish it were the same way here." In response to these comments, a boy who had been in residence for three and a half months pointed out to this boy,

"The trouble with you is you don't know how to stand on your own two feet. You want a list of rules because you don't know how to make your own decisions. I'll bet if you knew what the rules were around here you'd break every one of them behind everybody's back. I know, when I first came to Highfields, I didn't know what was going on either, but I learned after making a lot of mistakes that you don't need a lot of rules because I learned how to stay out of trouble. Besides, if you don't break any rules around here, you never get any problems and, if you never get any problems, you never learn anything. I don't think it would make any difference to you if you had a list of rules, anyway."

There are two general consequences for violating rules at Highfields. One of them was instituted at the request of the cottage parents, who felt that they needed some measure of control over the boys. What they wanted was an opportunity to give boys extra work to do whenever they failed to carry out their assignments. Out of this experience, there has emerged the concept of "hours in the pit." This is a generalized term which refers to extra work during leisure hours. Usually the cottage supervisor will give a boy one or more "hours in the pit." On extreme occasions, they will give a boy a day or a week in "the pit." More often than not a boy will work off his hours digging a garbage pit. Disposal of waste at Highfields consists of putting garbage in holes in the ground that are dug by boys who have "hours in the pit." Of course, a supervisor may decide that a boy should work off his hours around the house, either cleaning pots, scrubbing walls, raking leaves, or cutting the grass. Many times in the heat of a conflict situation, one of the cottage parents may give a boy six "hours in the pit" depending upon how he feels about the situation. Later on, he or she may decide to give the boy credit for six hours for doing a particular job which requires only one hour.

From time to time, a small group of boys gets concerned about numerous, excessive violations of rules and decides to deal with the situation as a group. This group's concern for violations is illustrated in the situation which is described below.

During the first meeting Eddie said that he wanted to discuss with the group the problem of how to stop the boys from gambling around the house. He explained that quite a few boys were gambling a great deal lately and that he felt we ought to stop it because it was wrong and also because some boys were going to get into some serious trouble over it. The group spent the entire meeting trying to determine ways of dealing with this problem. At the end of the meeting which was dominated largely by Brian and David, it was decided to discuss this problem with the members of the second group because as Stanley said, "We can't make decisions about the boys in the second meeting without talking to them about it." They decided then to ask the other boys if they would be willing to have a general meeting at the end of their own meeting that night.

About 9:35 P.M., just as the second group was ending its session, the members of the first group came running down the hall and knocked on the door. They came in and the general meeting began.

Brian asked Able whether he thought boys ought to be sent back to court if they were caught gambling. Bob smiled and shrugged his shoulders. I said, "Before we ask Bob about it it seems to me we should tell him what is going on. After all he doesn't know what we were talking about in the first meeting." Brian then said that was true and he would explain the situation. He said, "In our meeting we were trying to figure out some way to stop gambling around the house. It seems there are 5 or 6 boys who do all the gambling. Our group came up with a few suggestions. One of them was that we ought to send the boys who were caught gambling back to court and in that way it would stop the gambling." Paul interrupted and said the group had other suggestions as giving a boy extra "hours in the pit." Joe said, "We also decided maybe an extra K.P. would do the trick." Brian felt the group ought to vote on whether or not the boys ought to go back to court. Several of the boys agreed. Brian then went around the room starting out with Able. In reply Able said, "Pass me up, I don't know what to say because I don't gamble very much myself." Tom said, "I think that's kinda rough sending a boy back to court for playing cards. After all, maybe the boys are just playing casino or pinochle and Mr. M—— comes around and sees you, you know he is going to think you are gambling. Just because you don't have money on the table doesn't mean you aren't gambling. I just don't know what to think. I'll just go along with the group." Billy looked up a little bewildered and said quietly, "I'll go along with the group too." Joe said he was in favor of sending boys back to court. John, who was standing up, said, "No, I don't think we ought to send boys back to court." Before John could finish talking, he was interrupted by David who said, "That's the only thing we can do. No matter what else we try it's just not going to work. Just giving boys 'hours in the pit' is a waste of time, besides the other idea that you give a boy an extra K.P. is going to foul up the schedule." Several boys, including Brian, Chips, Joe, and John, said that didn't make any difference, the schedule could always be changed. John said that "maybe if we give a boy Sunday K.P. that would help. Boy when you get through at night you are pooped. No guy would like to do K.P. on Sunday twice in a row." David interrupted and said, "That's just not going to work. Suppose Mr. M—— catches 3 boys gambling one day and then he catches the same 3 boys 3 days later. That means by the time the last boy finishes his second K.P. he will have to wait six weeks. By that time he might be getting ready to go home and he would have to wait the extra time. That just won't work." John nodded his head and said David was right. Stanley and Brian also agreed. Brian told David to let John express his opinion and not to change his mind for him. Then Brian urged John to continue. He began where he left off saying, "To me Highfields is a place where the boys are supposed to get some help. It seems to me that if you send him back to court and he goes to A—— you aren't helping him at all, you are punishing him. What kind of help is that? You ought to give a boy a chance. After all, that's why a judge sends a boy to Highfields." Chips said, "I think he is right. If a boy stops gambling at Highfields because he is afraid of going to court, sure he is going to stop but as soon as he gets out he is going to start in all over again. I just don't see how that's going to help any of us." Brian and Joe began talking at the same time. Brian shouted the loudest and was heard saying, "Yeah, but if a boy stops gambling at Highfields because of the threat of going back to court then he might get into the habit of not gambling. Then when he gets out he won't have to worry about it." Tom said, "That's bullshit, Brian, and you know it. Look at what happened to David. He knew he would go back to court if he didn't stop gambling but that didn't stop him did it? You know that's not going to work." John interjected saying, "I think the boys will stop gambling if Mr. E—— actually sends somebody back to court. Then the boys will see what it means and will stop, but telling them isn't going to make them stop." Several boys agreed saying that was true. Brian, Joe, and Able cited examples to show that in David's case this experience didn't prove to be very good. In reply David said to each of them he just didn't know about it. He added, "But I haven't gambled for a long time now." Joe said the idea which he had brought up in the meeting might be a good one. He said, "I said then we should appoint three boys each week to report to Mr. E—— who is gambling around the house." There was a moment of silence then several boys murmured disagreements with Joe. Brian pointed out that that wouldn't work because one of the boys who was gambling might be appointed to watch over the other boys, "besides that wouldn't prove anything insofar as the boys' problems were concerned. It would be like making a boy a policeman." The group continued to discuss this and other alternatives with Brian, John, Eddie, and Stanley doing most of the talking. Finally, Brian said, "We aren't getting anywhere this way. Let's vote what we are going to do. I think we should leave it up to Mr. E—— anyway." Then he proceeded to go around the room asking each boy how he felt about it. All of them agreed it should be left up to me. Then Brian turned to me and asked, "What are you going to do, Mr. E——?" I said, "When I catch somebody gambling you will find out what I am going to do." They filed out of the office.

Although the crisis which was involved in the situation described above was not resolved in a clear-cut way, it does illustrate how the boys at Highfields attempt to work out solutions for some of their difficulties in concert.

The second general consequence of violating rules at Highfields is to be returned to court for another disposition. This means that the boy is transported to the county from which he came to make another court appearance. This decision, which is the responsibility of the director, is made from time to time. The boys in residence are very much aware of this situation and occasionally they will caution other boys who repeatedly get into difficulties, "If you don't watch out, you will be sent back to court." The seriousness of this situation is generally accepted, because to many of the boys it means going to the reformatory. In a sense, the knowledge that this is a possibility helps to create a measure of social control which is very important in the administration of the program. The reality of the reformatory oftentimes is sufficient to define the limits of conduct for the majority of boys. Since these limits are not the same for each boy, it is difficult to state the exact conditions under which a boy is returned to court for another disposition. However, boys who after a period of several weeks reveal an inability to profit from their experience, either by involvement in a series of assaultive acts which help create a state of fear in the house, or by participating in auto theft after running away, or by engaging in bizarre behavior, will probably be subject to return to court. When a boy is returned, a report and recommendation for disposition is made to the court. Many times, after evaluating the situation at Highfields, and particularly after attempting to forecast the possible impact of this court appearance on the boy himself as well as on the other boys in the house, a recommendation is made to the court that the boy be returned to Highfields. It should be noted that involvement in a single act is not sufficient cause to invoke this decision. Sometimes a small group of boys are involved in an incident and one or two boys are returned to court instead of all of them. For example, on one occasion three boys decided to hitch-hike home one Sunday afternoon to a city which was located about fifty miles from Highfields. Since they did not have to be in bed until about 10:00 P.M., they felt they could get a friend to return them to Highfields in time. However, as it turned out, they did not return until midnight. Of this group, one boy was returned to court. The other two boys felt that they should have been returned to court also, and attacked the director in the group sessions for not having done so. This was an opportunity to highlight the problems of each of the two boys and to compare them with the few possibilities that existed for helping the boy who was returned to court.

V

The Highfields Treatment Philosophy

WHILE WE WOULD PREFER IN THIS REPORT TO AVOID ANY SPECULA-
tion on the motives behind the delinquent act, and thus avoid
the knotty theoretical and practical problems involved in state-
ments on causation, our account would be incomplete without
some formulation around the basic problem that any effective
program to change attitudes is dependent upon; namely, a reasonably accurate conception of exactly what it is we wish to
change and in what direction we wish change to occur. In regard
to these issues, rather than make an attempt to explain delinquent conduct, our answer lies in Highfields' response to the
kinds of problems that the boys present at the project. These
problems seem to stem from the boys' conception of self and
others as hostile, aggressive, inadequate persons, and as "hipsters," "wise guys," "squares," and "suckers." The Highfields
program is organized to change and modify these distorted images
of self and other people. The structure attempts to bring an
awareness of the direct relationship between the learning tasks
at the project and the immediate psychological problems of the
residents, with a conviction that application in carrying out these
learning tasks will have a direct and positive effect on the amelio-
ration of these problems. These objectives, we hope, become realities in the lives of the boys in residence as a result of their intimate contacts with the Highfields social system that is maintained
by the technique of guided group interaction.

The usage patterns of the Highfields social system are based on the assumption that youthful offenders need an informal, easy, educational experience in a type of social world.[14] The important basic values in the Highfields social world are security, flexibility, and the absence of punitive or counter-aggressive attitudes on part of staff members.

Highfields is organized to meet the boys' need to feel that it exists to help them during a troubled period in their lives. The emphasis has been to organize and develop a total situation designed to accept and understand the "tough guys," "wise guys," "bad boys," and others, with their present attitudes and ways of relating to others. There is no magic in the proceedings of arrest, detention, or court hearing to transform a confused, anxious, bitter, rebellious delinquent into a boy without aggressions or hostilities; and a necessary initial experience for him is to feel that Highfields does not expect to make him become, almost overnight, a "good boy." If the youthful offender feels he must suddenly become something to get along in a world he has been compelled to enter, experience indicates that he becomes even more anxious, confused, and bitter. Take such a simple matter as eating. Some of the boys who enter Highfields have seldom, if ever, had the opportunity to enjoy a family meal. One such boy was an aggressive, impulsive seventeen-year-old lad who had been engaging in crime almost as a day-by-day occupation for two years prior to residence. This boy had been living in the streets continuously for five years, and at school was a truant and troublemaker. He graduated from selling papers and shining shoes to shoplifting and stealing automobile hubcaps. From this he moved into auto larceny and rolling drunks. He did not have any conception of how people are supposed to behave at a family meal, and would stand up, reach over the table, pile up his plate, and use his fingers instead of knives and forks during the meal. If he had met inflexible rules and regulations around behavior in the dining room, the chances are that instead of feeling High-

---

[14] Education is used here in the sense of comprehending all the experiences an institution can bring into the lives of the persons who live in it.

fields was designed to help him, his feelings of incompetence
would have been intensified. Since he was given the opportunity
to learn, from experiences with both staff and boys, the greater
satisfactions that come from conforming to certain basic rules,
he gradually learned to change his style of eating. When he departed from Highfields, while still not an ideal dinner compan-
ion for Emily Post, his eating habits were reasonably acceptable.
This example is used to illustrate the firm conviction of the Highfields project that youthful offenders need to work up to equality
with the outside world by a gradual promotion to those standards,
and not by the creation of special standards.

At Highfields, the emphasis has been to create situations where
boys can make choices from several possible ways of behaving and
then feel secure enough to discuss their particular choices. It cannot be emphasized too strongly that during residence all boys are
given opportunities to make choices in situations as much as
possible like those they will meet in the community. After making
their choices, opportunities to discuss them helps in the learning
of new social roles. It should also be pointed out that the emphasis is on their social roles in relation to one another rather than
to staff members. For instance, at Highfields, it is relatively simple
to steal food from the kitchen. While stealing from the kitchen
is disapproved of by both boys and staff, if a boy steals he is not
punished. Instead, he is given the opportunity to discuss this
behavior with both adults and peers. Since at one time or another
practically every boy in residence steals, and the tradition has
developed that it is all right to talk this over with the other boys
and the adults at the project, most of the boys will discuss such
an act. Needless to say, this talking it over with both adults and
peers can be a rewarding experience for all.

Flexibility is another indispensable element in the total educational atmosphere developed at Highfields. "Permissiveness" is
not used because of the possibility of suggesting the absence of
structure. As Kenneth Pray pointed out, "There is no absolute
freedom. There must be structure or authority, defining and enforcing the necessary limits upon individual person responsibility
and conduct, as a condition of social co-operation and as an in-

dispensable basis of any kind of life in any society." At Highfields the goal has been to develop a structure firm enough to give support and flexible enough to give scope to the boy's individuality. Frequently our boys have lived in a world filled with the "you mustn'ts" so delightfully expressed in one of Lewis Carroll's poems.

> 'What may I do' at length I cried,
> Tired of the painful task.
> The teacher quietly replied and said,
> 'You must not ask.'

A world of "you must not" will be challenged by the adolescent, and he will be in more-or-less constant conflict with it. This world orders and forbids, and from his point of view its rules and regulations may have little meaning. He may conform and be coerced into saying, "Yes, sir," but opportunities for him to work out his own rules and regulations are necessary. Consequently, at Highfields, there is not a conventional system of rewards and punishments. It is also important to have as few rules and regulations as possible and not permit them to become fixed, as a result of experience, in a tradition. Therefore, the rules for discipline are simple, easy for all to understand, and include only those which are essential for the maintenance of order. As David Wills observed, "This discipline is conceived as a framework on which to hang the routine services of a community—a device for seeing that those things are done which in any society must be done—that food is made available, cleanliness maintained, health preserved, and the rights of the individual to go about his lawful occupations upheld." This type of discipline is not conceived as character training.

For a community like this to function, it is necessary that all the people who live in it work toward attitudes of greater understanding of one another. It is as important for the boys to understand one another as it is for the staff to understand the boys, or the boys the staff. In this community, people must live together, share experiences, and know one another as persons. The social distance that separates the staff and boys cannot be enforced by rules and regulations, but must be inherent in their reciprocal roles. If the boy can test the adult role, and if he finds it satisfying, he can then, with more knowledge and understanding, accept the adult as a member of the community instead of as a hostile, threatening figure. Consequently, the boy's hostile and aggressive impulses toward both adults and peers are lessened, and he is able to turn to them for guidance and encouragement. In such a situation, there is little need for formal efforts to indoctrinate others, and instruction is by example, not exhortation.

We believe this type of project-design contains what we consider the basic elements indispensable to any program aimed at changing the attitudes or shaping the behavior of delinquent boys. The person must somehow be brought to an awareness that his difficulties are related to motives and patterns of perception within himself. His attempts to account for these difficulties by blaming a hostile or unfavorable human environment must be analyzed as deriving at least in part from a natural human tendency to avoid guilt and self-rejection. He must be assisted in gaining an awareness and a motivation for taking present initiative toward change or growth within himself, and he must be shown the fruitlessness of evading this responsibility by futile attempts to change merely his environment.

This assistance toward understanding comes about through some relationship with the therapist (or therapeutic situation) in which the individual actually attempts to make his faulty modes of perception and behavior work. Repeated demonstrations of this failure may be necessary before he is able to abandon them. It is important that these failures be not interpreted by him as indicating that he is a worthless or helpless person.

Finally, the individual must be provided with opportunities for the learning, testing, and fixating of newer, more effective modes of perceiving and relating to his human environment. As these new patterns emerge and are found rewarding in terms of increased success in relations with the self and others, they tend to become more and more established in the individual's total pattern of adjustment.[15]

---

[15] McCorkle and Korn, "Resocialization Within Walls," *Annals*, May 1954, p. 97.

As mentioned previously, the guided group interaction program at Highfields grew out of the development and use of group psychotherapeutic techniques during the Second World War in the processing of military offenders at the Fort Knox Rehabilitation Center to determine whether or not they should be restored to duty. There, under the leadership of Dr. Alexander Wolf, a comprehensive group therapy program that embraced all aspects of institutional living was initiated. This program was further implemented by the work of Dr. Joseph Abrahams and Dr. Lloyd W. McCorkle. This program has been described and its effectiveness has been evaluated.[16]

After the war, a number of correction institutions developed group activities programs which they referred to as group therapy. In a survey conducted in 1950 of 312 penal and correctional institutions, 39 responding institutions reported having a "group therapy" program. In addition, several indicated a willingness to include one in their treatment efforts. However, the same survey revealed that correctional institutions apparently responsive to the universal tendency to be fashionable had merely redesignated social and other types of group activities as group therapy. This was clearly indicated in the responses: 75 percent of the institutions incorporated group therapy into such activities as occupational therapy, activity and orientation programs. Only 25 percent of the institutions reported that group therapy as such was considered a part of a general psychotherapy program. Also in correctional institutions, 58 percent of the therapists or leaders were trained as teachers, occupational therapists, counselors, and educational directors. This survey revealed that correctional institutions relied on a lecture-discussion method, with only 9 percent reporting a psychoanalytic approach.[17]

In the development of the New Jersey group therapy programs at the training school and reformatory level started in 1947, it was felt advisable to differentiate clearly between this type of group

---

[16] J. Abrahams and L. W. McCorkle, "Group Psychotherapy on Military Offenders," *Am. J. Sociol.*, March 1946; idem: "Group Psychotherapy at an Army Rehabilitation Center," *Dis. Nerv. System*, February 1947.

[17] L. W. McCorkle "Present Status of Group Therapy in United States Correctional Institutions," *International Journal of Group Psychotherapy*, 3:79–87, 1953.

activity and other forms of group psychotherapy. In the first presentation of the New Jersey experiment in 1948, it was pointed out that "to avoid confusion with the use of group psychotherapy as practiced by psychiatrists, and to avoid any implication that all inmates are mentally abnormal and unbalanced, we decided to call the application of group therapy principles to inmates 'guided group interaction.' "[18]

As the title guided group interaction suggests, the therapist is active in the group discussion, especially in the initial sessions, and plays a critical, supportive, guiding role throughout the course of its history. Also implied in the title is the fact that the major emphasis is on the group and its development rather than on an attempt at exhaustive psychoanalysis of individuals in the group. "Guided group interaction," like all correctional techniques, makes assumptions about the kinds of socializing experiences delinquents need and can use if they are to achieve their usefulness as responsible citizens. It assumes the delinquent will benefit from a social experience where, in concert with his peers and the leader, he can freely discuss, examine, and understand his problems of living, without the threats that had been so common in his previous learning experiences. It further assumes that the mutual "give and take" of group discussion stimulates the delinquent to some understanding of the relationship between what takes place in this learning situation and his immediate problems of living. Therefore, the relationships encountered and the material discussed must be felt by the participant as making some contribution to his critical struggle for adjustment.

If participants are not degraded or excluded from the group because of their impulsive, aggressive behavior, the "group climate" must be lenient, accepting, and structured to give support to all. Freedom must exist for each participant to evolve his own role in the group and to learn to understand his present role; and opportunities must exist to develop new roles. This type of group

---

[18] F. L. Bixby and L. W. McCorkle, "A Recorded Presentation of a Program of Guided Group Interaction in New Jersey's Correctional Institutions," *Proceedings of the Seventy-eighth Annual Congress of Correction of American Prison Association, 1948.*

activity requires an easy, informal atmosphere where members are equals and where democratic social controls evolve out of interaction and increased understanding. It is inevitable, if these goals are reasonably achieved, for free emotional expressions to follow with the characteristic modes of adjustment of all participants exposed to one another and the therapist. In this process the participant's conception of self and others and the historical origin of these concepts are, through group discussion, related to his modes of adjustment.[19]

Groups of this type do not suddenly come into being because some person decides to form them. Rather, as a result of interaction and communication, members develop ways of relating to one another which make possible the analysis of behavior patterns. This process seems to follow an established pattern. Since the leader is, to the boy, a member of what frequently seems to him a hostile and unfriendly world, the boy is usually guarded and suspicious in his initial responses at the group sessions. As group members test the leader's role, hostilities and aggressions are directed at the world in general, at the administration of criminal justice in particular, and, somewhat later, at the leader. Behavior becomes disorderly, discussions aimless, and it might seem to the outsider that little, if anything, is accomplished. In time, the behavior of the group becomes more orderly, and the group supports and reinforces the leader's earliest definition of the therapy situation. There is some examination and analysis of the testing operations of the group and individual members of the group. When the group participants have satisfied themselves about the therapist, they test one another in a similar manner. If the anxieties and resistances have been adequately handled at each stage of the group's development, warm, friendly relationships replace earlier aggression and hostility. Concepts like "make progress," "help one another," and "he has a problem" give the group interests and goals which help to hold members together in a spirit of friendship and respect for the dignity of one another's personalities. Under the guidance of the leader, the group

---

[19] L. W. McCorkle, "Group Therapy in Treatment of Offenders," *Federal Probation*, December 1952.

freely discusses and examines the why's and wherefore's of their
stay at Highfields in relation to their patterns of adjustment. The
reward for their effort is twofold: They improve their prospects
of return to regular probation supervision, since a degree of self
understanding is a prerequisite; and they enjoy the personal
interplay of discussion.

The above description suggests some of the major problems
encountered in the establishment of "guided group interaction"
programs in the unique correctional environment. When the
free community and the correctional community are compared as
the immediate external situations for group therapy, certain
striking differences appear. An analysis of these differences, especially in terms of their negative aspects, would appear essential
prior to the setting up of therapy groups in the controlled social
ferment which constitutes a correctional institution. It is a universal observation that therapeutic changes in the personality
are accompanied by increased anxiety and tension. In the various
stages of the group history, the individual is subjected to experiences increasingly threatening to his established self-image. The
deep-rooted defenses of the inmate are pierced and he frequently
emerges from the sessions in a temporarily "crippled state" pro-
duced by the destruction of a previously important prop of the
self.

At this point, the striking difference between the correctional
institution and the external community as a setting for group
therapy is seen. The patient emerging from the therapist's office
on the outside can, in a sense, lose himself in a multiplicity of
noncritical interpersonal situations. Thus, the more "anonym-
ity" the external community provides, the greater are its shock-
absorbing potentials. For the person outside there are more
places to hide and lick wounds, and more ways to distribute
compensatory reactions to the inevitable initial feelings of personal devaluation. One of the supportive conditions of group
therapy on the outside is the patient's ability to escape from the
group. In the correctional institution, however, the inmate cannot
really leave the group. He is involved in numerous other activities
and living experiences with the same people with whom he has

shared intimate revelations, frequently against his will and in spite of all attempts at control and disguises. These individuals include his peers, his competitors, his enemies, or friends of his enemies—persons continually on the watch for signs of weakness or vulnerability.

The inmate, especially one of high status—and the higher the status the greater need for the emotional breaking down in most cases—has one of two unhappy alternatives at this point. The more healthy of these alternatives is to abandon his compensatory defenses and accept the more realistic image of himself. But this ideal alternative has many difficulties in correctional institutions where the wearing of socially appropriate masks is frequently the condition of personal survival. The individual who has committed himself to an aggressive leadership role has inevitably made enemies of those aspiring to a similar role and, like the despot in a feudal society, he can abandon his status only at his peril. Yet, these individuals are at the same time the most appropriate targets of an ambitious therapy program, since they form the major psychological supports of the antisocial inmate community.

This condition almost inevitably predisposes the inmate of high status under therapeutic attack to adopt a less healthy but more immediate comforting adjustment of aggressive compensation. This adjustment is full of danger to other inmates toward whom the inmate now feels it necessary to reassert his threatened role. Another aspect of this situation is presented by the previously low-status inmate who has gained strength from the group experience as a result of measuring himself against the high-status figure under attack. Where the latter is confronted with the painful prospect of a world to lose, the former is powerfully tempted by the prospect of a new world to win.

In this way, the therapeutic group in the correctional institution, if it is to be effective, must take the risk of becoming a manufactory of human projectiles let loose in a social situation which already has all the aspects of a human arsenal. It is therefore the moral obligation of the therapist to consider very carefully the serious question of the adequacy of the control elements in the institution, and the extent to which these are able to cope with the multiple tensions which will be generated. Failure to anticipate the effects of this added source of instability in an already inherently unstable situation will defeat the objectives of the program.[20]

Guided group interaction sessions, in which all of the boys in residence engage, provide stability to the project and are the medium through which the boys come to grips with their problems. There are in operation, at all times, two groups, the "old group" and the "new group." The former meets at 7:00 P.M., the latter at 8:30 P.M. Since membership in these groups is based entirely upon date of arrival, "old group" members have been in residence the longest. When most of the old boys have left, and enough new boys have arrived to form a therapy group, the meeting times are changed so that the new group automatically becomes the "old group" and their meeting begins at 7:00 P.M. This procedure has the effect of making these boys feel that, "we're getting ready to go home." Of course, it serves also to create a rivalry between the two groups.

When a new boy arrives, he is assigned to the "old meeting." Sometimes, he is the first member of a new group, other times he joins three or four other new boys to form the nucleus of a new group, or he becomes the last boy to join a new group; every group is closed to new members when it reaches a certain size, usually eight to ten boys. Every group, therefore, has a history of its own, for it has a beginning and an end. Since new boys are assigned to the "old meeting," they have an opportunity to witness and get involved in the discussions of the "old boys" and thereby learn by a process which can be likened to that of participant observation. In this way, too, they are oriented not only toward the techniques of participating in the group sessions but also toward Highfields as a whole, because it is in these sessions that the significance of Highfields becomes apparent. Through the process of informal orientation, every group is able to inter-

---

[20] L. W. McCorkle, "Guided Group Interaction in Correctional Setting," *International Journal of Group Psychotherapy*, Vol. IV, No. 2, April 1954, pp. 199–203.

nalize the culture of Highfields and, also, to transmit this culture in turn to other new groups as they arrive.

These group meetings are held every evening of the week except Thursday and Saturday. Thursday evenings are difficult periods for many boys simply because, as they claim, "There's nothing to do and no place to go." Of course, for the staff it is an excellent opportunity to observe the interaction between the boys in terms of the kinds of cliques that form, the games they play, the fights and arguments they are continually creating, their thefts from the refrigerator and from each other, the card playing and the gambling that inevitably follows every card game, the boys that are isolated from the others by choice or otherwise, and other activities.

The guided group interaction sessions permeate all phases of life at Highfields, whether it is work or play, fighting or arguing, eating or walking, and sometimes sleeping. On one occasion, a boy complained in a meeting that "A guy can get into trouble at Highfields even when he is sleeping." Before going to sleep he had talked a friend into throwing water at another boy. The next evening, when this incident was discussed by the group, he made his complaint. The pervasive impact of the group sessions is best illustrated by an expression that is commonly employed both in jest and in sincerity, that "everything a boy does can be a problem, you can't avoid problems around here. If you fool around, you got a fooling around problem, if you don't fool around, you get a being too quiet problem, what is a guy supposed to do anyway, you can't win."

Of course, the effect of a boy's experience in a group session is felt in the community as well. It can be seen when a boy describes his relations with the probation officer, his parents, the police at home, and his gang. In describing a furlough, one boy related an incident that took place with a friend of his. He said, "This place is getting me. A friend of mine asked me if I wanted to go to the show with him. Without thinking I asked him why. He looked at me kind of funny. Later on we were talking about what he was doing. He mentioned everything but work. When I asked him why he wasn't working, he looked at me again and he said,

'What's the matter with you, you going nuts, every time I say something you ask me why, now you want me to go to work. Boy you better forget about that place. You're going crazy!'" Of course, there are other boys who assert that they forgot all about Highfields during their furloughs because "they were glad to get away and forget about problems altogether."

Since the guided group interaction sessions are at the core of the project design, a summary of one group is presented. This group had its first session on August 25, 1950, and all the members were released prior to December 25, 1950. One boy, Bob, was returned to court as unsuitable and committed to a reformatory.

————————

Group Members

1) Joe—a dull, immature, dependent 17-year-old, is the son of a drunken, brutal Italian immigrant father and an indulgent mother. A product of a broken home in the Newark slums, he was admitted to Highfields after a street fight in which he was accused of violently assaulting another boy.

2) Bob—an intelligent, withdrawn, aggressive 17-year-old boy who remained inaccessible to the program at Highfields, is the son of a vague, inadequate mother and an insane father. He was received at Highfields after study and classification at the diagnostic center where he was admitted for auto larceny.

3) Pete—an 18-year-old, talkative, sophisticated delinquent who was admitted to Highfields after his first court appearance for armed robbery.

4) Steve—a 17-year-old, aggressive, quiet, polite boy with a long delinquency career, his mother died in childbirth, and his father is a former alcoholic.

5) Harry—an open, out-going adolescent who constantly ran away from his home which was characterized by constant conflict between himself and his parents. His poor school adjustment, petty stealing, and undesirable associates, plus incorrigibility at home, brought him to Highfields.

6) Sam—a good-natured, dull, aggressive, immature 16-year-old, whose indulgent mother and demanding father felt he was "be-

yond control." This, plus inability to adjust at school, constant truancy, petty stealing, undesirable companions, and roaming the streets, was responsible for his admittance to Highfields.

7) Larry—a 17-year-old, frightened, anxious boy who was the son of a Chinese-Polish mother and a Philippine father who separated prior to his birth. He spent his childhood with a Polish grandmother in Chicago, but moved at age nine to a Michigan Chinatown where he lived with his mother and stepfather. When he was fourteen his mother died and he moved to Newark to live with his father and stepmother. He associated with a gang of young Italian delinquents and soon appeared in juvenile court for larceny. He violated probation by becoming involved in gang street fights and was admitted to Highfields.

8) Gus—a friendly, confused, anxious, rebellious 17-year-old, is the son of a rigid, domineering, aggressive mother and a hard-working, indifferent father. He was admitted to Highfields after several court appearances for larceny and use of drugs.

August 28, 1950.

The boys played a ball game in the early evening with the New Jersey Neuro-Psychiatric Institute, and Joe, although he struck out at bat, made a spectacular catch in center field and led the victory parade back to Highfields.

At the start of the session, Joe talked about the ball game, "our wonderful team," and his skill as a ball player. Pete, the outstanding player from Highfields, looked disgustedly at Joe while he talked about the game.

The boys discussed why it is that people think they are not going to do something and, later on, do it. This discussion resulted from Sam telling about how he promised himself that he would stay awake during the day and sleep at night. He said that even at Highfields he found himself taking a nap after work and almost missing supper. Steve related this to his stealing and said he has wondered many times "why I ever did it." The boys all started to talk about why people steal, and Joe said it was a case of "bad companions." Roy said he couldn't understand why he stole the things he did unless it was because he got "a kick out of it." He said the things had little value to him and, therefore, the only reason he could think of was the thrill. Steve said his stealing was related to running around with a gang of kids whom he liked and wanted to like him, and so when they stole, he stole. When he talked about this, he did not try to put the responsibility on the other boys and said that as he looked at it, it was hard to say any one person was any more responsible than the others. This made Pete a little uneasy since he consistently blames his troubles on his friends who are in the reformatory. Pete, when asked what he thought about this, said, "I guess you want something and you go around with guys that will help you get it." When asked what it was he wanted, he replied that he needed money and decided to get it "the easy way." One of the boys asked him what he needed money for, and he replied, "You'll all laugh if I tell you, but I wanted it to get married." None of the fellows laughed, and one boy said, "That's as good a reason as any."

Sam went on to describe some of his delinquencies and told of stealing automotive equipment from trucking concerns. He gave as his reason for this behavior, "They have plenty of money." Larry thought his stealing was tied up with his wish to have fancy clothing, and Harry said that while he never stole very much, when he did steal, it was with a gang, and he did it because everybody else did. Joe surprised everyone by saying he had never stolen anything in his life. When he said this, all the boys roared, and Pete said it was impossible. Joe defensively told a long story about a man he knew who got shot while stealing, and this had been so impressive that he was never going to steal. He concluded by saying that all people who steal are very bad, and they should be locked up for long periods of time, and would probably never reform. At this, all the boys became quite angry, and one said, "If you go around beating people up, you might kill them, and I think it's worse to hit a guy who can't defend himself than it is to steal from somebody."

At the close of the session, Joe demanded that he be permitted to go to town to buy shoes. When it was pointed out to him that he had had several opportunities to get shoes while he was in town with Mr. L——, he said he didn't like those shoes and he wanted to go to Trenton or Newark to buy them. When told that transportation was not available and, therefore, it would be impossible, he became upset, said we wanted miracles around Highfields, and that he was "sick of the damn joint."

September 22, 1950.

The group was minus Joe who had a week-end furlough and Sam who was on K.P. The boys just sat quietly, and when the leader asked if they had anything they wanted to talk about, they did not reply. After a few minutes, it was suggested that since they didn't have anything to talk about, they might want to leave. None of the boys made any effort to go, and when asked if they didn't want to leave, they smiled self-consciously, and Steve said, "I guess not, or we'd leave." One of the other boys said, "We're waiting for something to talk about." When asked if they could think of any reason why they had so much difficulty talking, Pete said, "It's now time to look at the other side of the coin." Steve added, "We have to face the facts of why we got in here. That's the thing we have to talk about." Bob said, "That's easier said than done." When asked if there was any connection between their awkward starts and what Bob had just said, Gus replied, "You mean we don't want to talk about the real reasons we got in here, and we don't say anything." Most of the boys smiled and shook their heads in the affirmative. Pete said, "I'm ready to face the facts," and turned to Steve and asked him if he was ready to "face the facts." Steve said he was. Pete then went around the room and asked each boy if he wanted to "face the facts." They all replied in the affirmative with the exception of Bob who pulled his chair off a bit from the rest of the group and just nodded his head.

Harry, after this was over, said, "Tell me why I got in here." The boys said, "We don't know much about you except what we have seen around here." Steve suggested that since Harry was always running away from home, apparently he didn't like his home. Harry said he didn't like his home, hated his father whom he described as being disinterested in him. He told about his father with a great deal of emotion, and told how he had re-

marked to some of his friends, that, "Harry is no damn good."
Steve said this makes a kid feel "shut out" from the rest of the
family and causes him a lot of trouble. Pete said, "If your parents
treat you like that, you have to run away or get in some kind of
trouble." Harry told of the problems with his brothers who are
his parent's favorites. As he put it, "They always got away with
things, but I never could." He told how both his mother and
father preferred his older and younger brothers and how he became interested in mechanics in an effort to excel and be "better
than my brothers." Gus became very talkative, told Harry about
his case, and how they were alike in every respect, except, instead
of having the most trouble with his father, he had more difficulty
with his mother. Both of the boys cited numerous specific cases
to support their opinions that they were less liked by their parents than their brothers. Both of the boys described how they
felt "left out" of the family and their reactions to this—in Harry's
case, running away, in Gus' case, stealing from his brother. As
the meeting progressed, it became a conversation between Gus
and Harry with Steve and Pete less active, and Bob and Larry
off in a corner. Neither Bob nor Larry made any effort to get into
the conversation. Both acted bored, pretended to sleep, but made
enough noise occasionally to attract the interest of the others.

As Gus and Harry went on in their discussion, they started to
discuss what you could do about this problem when you leave
Highfields. Gus said, "It's best to ignore it." Steve entered the
conversation and said he thought it was impossible to ignore it
and this was easy to say while at Highfields, but hard to do when
home. Harry agreed, telling how he had tried to ignore it many
times, but later on, he would get so angry that he had to do something. Gus laughed, said that was true for him, but, "Maybe if
you got to understand others, you could do it." Harry said he
always felt better when he was staying with the family of his boss
because, "If he treated his children better than me, I can always
say he should treat them better." Harry then went on in some
detail to describe his attachment to a 26-year-old independent
truck driver who had repeatedly befriended him. He said this
man was like a father and "willing to talk to you." He said he

would do anything for this man, and after his release from High-fields he hoped to be able to work for this man again.

Steve said it was pretty easy to take advantage of Harry, that he was too easy-going. This observation was the result of Harry's telling of what he would do for his friend. Steve expressed the opinion that this friend had used Harry for his own selfish purposes. Harry, when asked if he thought of himself as too easy to get along with, flushed and said it might be true. He went on to say that he did find it hard to say no when others asked him to do things. Gus said that he thought Harry was "too generous" and that people would take advantage of him. Gus said that Harry did all these things because he wanted people to like him. This upset Harry, who replied that he wasn't "That bad. I can say no and there are a lot of people I won't do anything for." Pete said he thought Harry was "very generous." The other boys described Harry as being "friendly and loyal." Pete said he didn't think Harry was really as much of a "square" as he did at first, and that "he's the kind of fellow you can depend on."

The meeting ended, but before the boys left, it was summarized and they were asked if they could think of any reasons why, as the meeting progressed, only Harry and Gus were active. Gus said he guessed it was because "it was about our problem." When asked if they could think of any reasons why Bob and Larry couldn't join in the group discussion and why both Pete and Steve had less and less to say as the meeting went on, the boys seemed surprised, and Pete said, "I can't understand why Bob didn't get in the meeting, but some things Harry said bothered me."

September 27, 1950.

Pete started the group meeting with a number of questions about the laundry. After these were answered, the group decided how they were going to mark their laundry. There was a silence that lasted approximately three minutes. The boys looked at one another, smiled good-naturedly. Finally, Gus said he would like to go on discussing his problem with Bob. Gus said he had been thinking about how Bob was like his brother, and he could think of a lot of reasons that hadn't been mentioned in the last meeting.

As he went on, he described both his brother and Bob as quasi-superior, argumentative persons who always "pick on me." Gus said, "Even if I do get mad at them I like them, and I want to be around them." Gus told how his mother would always take his brother's part in their arguments and said, "She was always chiming in, and even after my brother forgot about it, she would keep it up." Gus described his father as being much more fair, and less obvious in preferring his older brother. Gus told how his older brother criticized him about "all sorts of things," his feelings of anger and resentment about this, and how he would keep these feelings inside until "I couldn't hold them anymore."

Throughout all this, Bob would occasionally insert a remark to the effect that, "He does similar things to me. It's impossible for me to tell Gus anything." All the boys discussed criticism of family members and how they responded to it. Pete said his older brothers "were always telling me what to do, but I thought I was just as good as any of them so I didn't pay any attention." Harry, with considerable feeling, told of his experiences with an older brother who, as he put it, "always found fault with the way I did things, and couldn't do them half as well himself." Joe said most of his brothers were "nice fellows" who didn't criticize him, just wanted to help him. Bob stated, "My brother and I have an understanding, he doesn't bother me, and I don't bother him. In a lot of ways, we're alike." The boys discussed why they were unable to accept or use the criticism and good advice of their older brothers and parents. Steve said, "It doesn't matter how much some people tell you something, and you may even know it's right, but you still don't listen." Most of the other boys agreed that it was true that most of the advice they had received had been good and that they wanted to follow it, but something always seemed to get in the way.

They then discussed criticism in the group and how the members felt about this. Several of the boys said that when other members criticized them, even if they felt the other boys were right, they had to argue "or get mad about it." Several of the boys gave illustrations of this from their experiences at Highfields. The boys agreed that this was true for most people, if you criticized them, they felt hurt and resentful. Sam said this wasn't true for him because when the boys criticized him, "At first I was upset. Later I could see it was for my own good and I think I have been getting along much better since we had that meeting." Joe said he didn't care if the fellows criticized him since, "They are trying to help me." All of the boys laughed at this, and Pete said, "Why doesn't he wise up?" Joe started to laugh, looked anxiously about and said, "I mean it."

The boys then discussed their reactions to criticism from people they liked. Harry told how he could accept criticism from his former employer whom he liked but could not from his father. The group agreed that they were able to accept and use more criticism in the group now because they had more feeling that the other boys were trying to help them. Gus said he didn't think Bob was always trying to help the other fellows when he criticized them. Bob smiled about this, said it was probably true, and looked at Sam and laughed. Bob said, "He feels that way about me, and lately I have just avoided trying to tell him anything." Sam smiled and said, "Bob's okay, but he's always using big words and trying to impress us." Most of the boys agreed, and Bob laughed and said it was probably true.

As the end of the hour approached, attention was called to Larry who had remained silent throughout the hour. Larry had pretended to sleep, slouched in his chair, trying to give the impression of ignoring what was going on. The group laughed and Steve said Larry probably liked his day-dreams better than the group. Larry smiled but gave no explanation for his behavior.

After the meeting, Larry asked if he could see the leader for a minute. He seemed upset, told the leader he was worried about his father, and how he was not able to get visits like the other boys. Larry asked if he might have his friends come and if he would be permitted to go out with them in their car like the other boys. When asked what he thought about this, he replied, "I can see why you would turn me down on the request. It might get everybody into trouble." He then asked if his friends brought his father to Highfields, would he be able to go out with them and his father. When told there wasn't any objection to this, he seemed pleased and asked if he could call his friends and ask them to bring his father up. When asked if he thought this was an emergency, he replied it wasn't, but he would like to speak to his friends. He finally said he would write a letter and ask his friends to bring his father to Highfields.

October 27, 1950.

The boys were quiet and orderly entering the room. Sam suggested the group should continue to discuss Pete. The group made a half-hearted attempt to start, but most of the boys lapsed into silence. In response to the observation that apparently they didn't want to talk about Pete but perhaps there was something else they wanted to talk about, several of the boys smiled.

When asked if they wanted to talk about Bob's leaving, all the boys entered into the discussion. (Bob was returned to court earlier that day because of his failure to adjust at Highfields.) Their comments were to the effect that it was a big surprise. Later, as they discussed their surprise, all the boys stated they had a feeling that Bob would have to be returned to court. Pete stated that Bob also knew that he was going to have to be returned to court and added, "He couldn't do anything about it." Pete continued by stating, "Bob had more problems than any of us, but he could never talk about his problems. He wanted more than any of us to be able to talk about his problems, but when the time came, he could not. That guy was a sad case. Bob told me he had been suspended from work at the Institute, and he knew if he continued, he would have to be returned to the court, still he couldn't help himself. He was like a guy going down hill and couldn't stop." Other members of the group were surprised when Pete told them that Bob had been suspended from work at the Institute. Pete said Bob had told only him about this. Sam said he could feel it coming, and that Bob was keeping other boys from making progress. The group paused to discuss this, and all of them, except Joe and Larry, expressed the opinion that Bob was a disruptive influence at Highfields. Larry asked if it wouldn't be possible for Bob to serve his time at the House of Detention, and then be released on probation without having to go to a reformatory. The boys were unanimous in saying that a reformatory would not help Bob.

The boys first started to talk about themselves in relation to Highfields and whether or not they might be returned to court. They needed reassurance that return to court was not just an arbitrary decision, and it was necessary to emphasize the point made by Pete earlier that Bob's relations at Highfields had been carefully explained to him and evaluated with him for a month prior to the final decision. Most of the boys repeated their opinion that Bob was causing too much trouble, both at the Institute and at the house, to be tolerated much longer. After saying this, they quickly added their hopes that he would not go to the reformatory. Steve stated that, to some extent, the entire group was to blame because, "We should have helped Bob more. We knew he had the problems that Pete was talking about, and yet we didn't make him talk about them at the group meetings and help him." Pete said that several times he felt he wanted to help Bob bring his problems to the surface but, "He had a way of twisting things around and putting you on the spot." Pete referred to the earlier group meeting in which he and Bob came close to having a fight. Pete said he felt a little guilty about not helping Bob because he was the person at the project who knew him best, and yet he was afraid to try because he felt it would make trouble between Bob and himself.

The group were informed that two of their members, Sam and Harry, were going to leave Highfields permanently on Sunday. Both boys were surprised by this information. Sam blushed, smiled, and said, "You mean I'm going to leave the day after tomorrow?" When told this was true he said that he was very happy but that he didn't think it would happen for several weeks. Harry said he was surprised, and said he thought maybe he would be here until Christmas. Most of the other group members were surprised, but all of them said that probably Sam and Harry would be able to get along after their release. Pete said, "They had little problems, and I think they will be able to get home in the evening on time, and neither one of them will start running away from home again." Steve stated that while he was happy for

Harry and Sam, he felt disappointed that he wasn't leaving because, "After all, we came here the same day." Larry seemed a little upset, but said he was glad for his friends. Joe hastened to assure everybody that he didn't have any feelings about the other boys' leaving although he has been at Highfields six weeks longer than either of them. When Joe said this, the other boys started to laugh, and finally Joe laughed and said he guessed he did "feel bad because I'm not going home." The other boys started to give Sam and Harry some advice and said they hoped they would see them in Newark after they were released. Several of the boys said that it would be tough on the football team to lose both Harry and Sam.

October 30, 1950.

The group meeting started with a statement by Pete that he wanted to discuss some trouble that he had had with Joe. He said that he and Joe had not been very good friends for the past three weeks, and that Friday night, it had reached a climax, and that he wanted to bring it out in the open. When the leader asked the boys what they thought the difficulty was, Pete said Joe bothered him, and Joe said Pete "picked on" him. All of the boys present got into the discussion. Gus said he thought Pete looked at Joe as a "jerk" and that Joe thought Pete was a "hipster." Since Joe wanted to be associated with Pete and he would have nothing to do with him, there had to be trouble between them. Steve said he thought Pete looked at Joe as a "punk" who is always trying to act tough, but wouldn't associate with him because to do so would mean Pete was not a "hipster." Larry said he agreed with Steve and Gus and, as he looked at it, Joe had done a lot of things that irritated Pete, and Pete did a lot of things that irritated Joe. Joe said that he liked Pete and wanted to be friendly with him, but Pete thought he was a "smart guy." Pete said that Joe had always bothered him a little bit, and he resented having Joe about always wanting to do things for him or give him things. Pete then went on to give several specific illustrations and mentioned that on one occasion, Joe gave him a shirt, frequently supplied him with writing paper, and, at various times, offered him money. Pete said he had been willing to take the shirt and writing paper, but had never taken any money from Joe. Gus said that in doing this, Pete was only behaving with Joe the way he had behaved with girls in the past, taking things from them, and later on pushing them around. Steve said that Joe's demands on Pete were such that he couldn't be friendly in spite of the gifts. Pete said that he felt funny when he took the things, and while he didn't want to take things from Joe and feel indebted to him, he did because, "I liked to have them." Later on, he described his feelings as wanting to be nice to Joe, but after a couple days giving up and again "picking on him" and doing things to get him angry.

Joe said that much of what the boys said was true, that he did make a lot of demands on Pete and, above all, he wanted to feel that Pete would leave him alone or, what is more important, be on his side. Joe spontaneously told the boys that in giving Pete things, he was behaving toward him as he did toward his father. Joe stated that Pete, like his father, would "pick on" him, say things to him to irritate him, and just as he gave his father money to leave him alone, he gave Pete gifts in the hopes that he would leave him alone. This admission on Joe's part surprised the other boys, and several of them stated that on several different occasions they had noticed that when anyone picked on Joe, he would later do something for them or offer them some gifts. Gus said this was the only way Joe could make friends, and as a result of this, he had acquired a reputation as a "ball buster." Joe said this was true, that both with his father and with others before coming to Highfields, he was willing to give them almost anything in the hopes that they would be friendly with him and include him in their activities. Joe went on describing how, although he disliked his father for things he did to him, he would nevertheless give him money. Joe said he resented very much having to give his father money, but it was "easier than having him pick on you or having him fight with my mother." Steve said that it looked as if Joe was behaving toward Pete as he did toward his father, and that he was having the same trouble as he did before.

Pete said that it was important that he and Joe get this thing straightened out because they would both meet people on the outside that would resemble one another for them. Joe said he liked Pete, hoped he would be his friend but at the same time, he resented him and his easy way of getting friends and how he was able to have the respect of all the boys without even trying. Larry said it was all Joe's fault, that he was constantly creating trouble for himself, and, "He has to learn that you can't push other people around." Gus and Steve said they thought Joe did this because he never was sure that either Pete or Larry liked him. Pete said this was true because several times Joe had told them he didn't like them. Joe protested that he did trust Larry but not Pete. Pete said he felt hurt when "Joe told Bob and Bill who aren't even in our group about himself," but was never willing to trust either the group or him with this knowledge. Joe protested that the only reason he included Bill in his confidence was because he happened to be around when he decided to tell his troubles to Bob. Joe went on talking about how he had many similar feelings toward Pete that he had toward his father, and several of his older brothers. In a pathetic manner, Joe described a lifetime of being "picked on" by others, especially members of his family. He went on to tell the boys that he never felt sure that others liked him, and since he did want them to like him, he would give them things.

The boys were quite impressed by Joe's statement, and hastened to assure him that they liked him and would like him even more if he would "stop his damn bragging." Pete went on to say that Joe's wish to do things for him would upset him, and several times he had to chase him away. Joe said this was true and he couldn't understand why he was always willing to do whatever Pete wanted. Gus and Steve started to give numerous illustrations of the way Joe would act around Pete. They told how he would hold a choice seat for him in the truck, give him his dessert, etc. The boys added that Pete would take these things, and later make a fool out of Joe. Pete agreed, and said he couldn't understand why he did it except that it irritated him to have Joe always interfering and wanting to do things for him. Pete said he now refused to permit Joe to do any more things for him, and the boys agreed that this has been true for the past several weeks.

Before the session ended the boys asked Gus what he got out of his furlough home. Gus laughed, said it was a lot of fun, and that he hated to come back. Gus told of missing the train although he was with his mother and girl friend at the station an hour and a half before train time. As Gus described it, he ran up the wrong stairs and by the time he got himself straightened out, the train was gone. He said he was upset about this, and his mother was very disturbed, criticized him for being so stupid, but his girl friend suggested that he call Highfields and tell us he would be on the next train. The boys all laughed and kidded Gus about not wanting to come back and making sure to miss the train. Gus agreed and told the boys how confused he became and the trouble he had finding the ticket office to buy his ticket. Gus said he knew he had to come back but he wanted to stay in Newark more than anything else in the world. The boys kidded about how nice it would have been if he hadn't found the ticket office because then he would never have had to return to High-fields. Gus smiled, said he guessed that was true, and it probably explained why he got lost and missed the first train.

November 8, 1950.

The boys had difficulty getting the meeting started. When asked if they had anything they wanted to discuss, nobody responded. The group sat silently for approximately ten minutes, and finally Joe said, "Let's talk about something." When it was suggested it might be a good idea if the group discussed why they were again finding it difficult to start, Steve said he didn't think he would have started the meeting even if the group had remained silent for an hour. Pete said he felt the same way. Gus said the silence bothered him, and it seemed like a waste of time to just sit. Gus said the group ought to talk about Pete and his problem.

Steve said he thought the reason Pete didn't talk was because the group didn't seem to be getting anywhere with his problems, and hadn't given him any answers. Steve said, "He feels let down." All of the boys laughed at this, and Pete shook his head in the negative. When asked if Pete didn't feel that way if there was anyone who did, Gus said, "That's the way Steve feels." Steve admitted that he did feel "let down" and for the last several weeks "I have had the feeling you let me down." Pete said he had a feeling that the leader didn't like him. He went on discussing this feeling and said, "From the first day we met, I had the feeling you didn't like me." As he talked about this, he qualified it with, "Maybe you like me at the group meeting, but other times you don't like me. I'll bet if we were working together some place, you wouldn't like me." When the other boys were asked what they thought of this, Steve said, "I don't have a feeling you don't like me, but there are times when I don't like you. I don't like you because instead of telling me the answer to my problem, you tell me to figure it out." Gus said this was the only way it could be, that there wasn't any answer to some problems. Steve agreed this might be true, but said he thought that the leader should be more help and, "Sometimes I have a feeling you don't give a damn."

Pete moved in at this point to discuss his feelings that the leader didn't have any confidence in him, and his feeling that the leader did not believe he was making progress. Gus and Steve picked this up and said that on several occasions the leader pointed out to Pete his lack of progress and probably "he is sore because he couldn't smooth-talk you." Gus started to laugh and told about how on one day, Pete describes the leader as a "great guy" and the next day, "a son-of-a-bitch." Pete admitted he did this, and said that when he returned from work at 5:00 P.M. he had a feeling of friendliness and warmth toward the leader, but after the meeting started, he found himself getting angry with him, and said, "I can't understand it, but sometimes I have the feeling you don't like me." All of the boys said they thought one of the reasons Pete felt that the leader didn't like him was because he hadn't granted him a furlough, and it was very difficult for him to see other boys who came to Highfields after him get furloughs. Pete said that this was true, and while he tried to convince himself that the leader was doing it for his own good, it just didn't seem that way. As he said this, he started to discuss his anxieties about his relationship to Highfields and the possibility that he might be returned to the court because, "I'm not making progress." As he talked about this, he was able to admit that during the first several months of his stay at Highfields, he decided that, "Anybody can do four months, and I'll pull my time the easy way." He said that as time went on, he found this more and more difficult, and is now making a sincere effort to improve. The other boys gave him a great deal of encouragement and support, assured him that he was making progress. Steve said, "He's not the same Pete." Gus claimed that Pete was more open and does less "smooth-talking." Pete went on to say that he had arrived at the conclusion that unless he made progress at Highfields, he might get into serious trouble after his return to Newark, and he wanted to do things that would help him be a success on probation.

The boys were asked if they could figure out any reasons why Pete would have these mixed feelings about him. Gus offered the explanation that probably the leader reminded him of someone that he likes and also dislikes. Steve said that was probably true because, "You remind me of my father, and I feel toward you the way I do toward him many times." Pete said he could not think of anybody that the leader reminded him of, and Gus suggested that perhaps the leader reminded him of a girl because his behavior in relation to him is frequently like the behavior he describes as being true of his past relationships with women. The boys then talked a little bit about how Pete "tried to smooth-talk" the leader but failed. The group said Pete always "smooth-talked" women. Pete helped the boys develop this by saying he wanted to feel dependent on the leader, but when he found himself doing this, he would become annoyed and irritated with himself and on these occasions, he would want to tell the leader "to go to hell." The boys gave several specific instances of Pete's dependence on the leader, and how he would become very angry when he treated him like the other boys, particularly if it was during a time when he had been praising the leader to other boys. All of the boys, including Pete, laughed about this, and Joe said he felt that way too, and started to talk about his present feelings toward the leader. Joe said he had a feeling he wanted to put something over on the leader before he left Highfields, and the other boys laughed and said that Joe wanted to prove to them before he departed that he was "smarter than M———." Gus said Joe was probably angry at himself for the way he acted at Highfields. Joe became a little upset at this, said it might be true but that, "I feel you helped me a great deal and I don't want to do anything to make you mad at me."

The boys returned to Pete and his mixed feelings about the leader. Gus said while he was at Highfields, he would have to learn to accept disappointments and not get angry at the leader. Steve said this was a hard thing to do especially "when you want to go home on a furlough." Gus agreed that this was true, described his own feelings that the leader didn't care for him when he felt he was denying his requests for a furlough. The leader called the boys' attention to the fact that the group has difficulty getting started, but after they get the meeting going, they have trouble bringing it to a close. Steve said he guessed this was because you find it hard to start talking, but after you get started, there are so many things you want to talk about, and there never seem to be answers to the things brought up in the group meetings.

VI

Evaluation of Highfields Residents

AT THIS POINT, AFTER FIVE YEARS OF OPERATION, THERE ARE STILL many open questions concerning just how and to what extent Highfields has justified the hopes which were responsible for its existence. However, to one set of questions, there are now some clear answers. We now know that it is possible to apply the techniques of group therapy for short periods of time in situations which conventionally would call for prolonged "reformatory" treatment. For many boys the outcome is helpful. The community is satisfied with the results. The staff find the experience as rewarding as the process is difficult.

This volume is an effort to record the philosophy underlying the treatment; to report, in relatively nontechnical fashion, what seems to be going on; and to suggest the areas in which more objective research and study may profitably be done.

In 1950 the Vincent Astor Foundation gave support to a research project designed to assess, more objectively than we have here attempted, the effects of Highfields. This project has been directed by Professor Ashley Weeks of New York University with advice from a Scientific Advisory Committee headed by Professor E. W. Burgess of the University of Chicago. That research, and other similar studies which we hope will follow, will ultimately provide fully adequate measures of Highfields' accomplishments. Meanwhile, we hope that this account of our own experience to date will provide a background of material against which more definitive studies may be planned.

97

During the first five years of its existence, several hundred boys were sent to Highfields. Who are these boys? What happened to them during their residence? What kind of adjustment did they make in the community after they returned to their homes? In this chapter we shall attempt to deal with some of these questions. In a subsequent chapter a comparative analysis is presented of the post-release adjustment of a selected group of Highfields graduates and parolees from the state reformatory.

The data that are presented here include the following: description of the boys and their adjustment at Highfields, and their adjustment in the community, including their probation officers' evaluation of them. The period under study was a five-year time-span from July 1950, when Highfields opened its doors to the first admission, through June 1955.

DISPOSITION OF THE POPULATION

Usually, in a conventional correctional facility, the inmates receive three types of dispositions: They are released on parole, discharged from the institution following the completion of their maximum sentences, or transferred to another correctional facility as a result of a warrant, extradition proceedings, or a classification decision. Boys who are released from Highfields receive various types of dispositions also. Chart 2 shows that as of June 30, 1955, the overwhelming majority of the boys—75.7 percent—were returned to the supervision of the several county probation departments, 18.6 percent were declared unsuitable for residence for one reason or another, and the remaining 5.7 percent were still in residence and had not yet completed their period of training.

Of the 317 boys who were admitted during the five-year period of this study, 199, or 62.8 percent, were still in the free community following their release, and 41, or 12.9 percent, were committed to another correctional facility after their release from Highfields. The latter group includes boys who were sentenced to a county jail for committing misdemeanors and other offenses as well as boys who were committed to a state correctional institution.

CHART 2

Disposition of Boys Admitted to Highfields 7/1/50–6/30/55
(left-hand numbers indicate percentages)

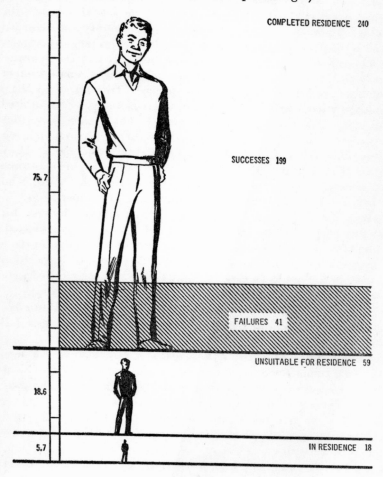

COMPLETED RESIDENCE 240

SUCCESSES 199

75.7

FAILURES 41

UNSUITABLE FOR RESIDENCE 59

18.6

5.7

IN RESIDENCE 18

ADJUSTMENT AT HIGHFIELDS

The 59 boys who were declared unsuitable for residence are included in five separate sub-categories. Thirty-four of them were "Returned to Court" for another disposition. Of this number, the judges committed 29 boys to the state reformatory and returned the remaining five boys to probation. In the second sub-category, "Runaways," nine were subsequently sentenced to the reformatory and two were returned to probation status. A small number of boys appear in the third sub-category, "Transferred to Diagnostic Center." Included in this group are five boys who exhibited serious psychopathological symptoms. It was decided that they required a period of observation and testing in a psychiatric setting, for which purpose the Diagnostic Center was designed. Only three boys required hospitalization for an extended period of time as a result of a serious illness or injury. At Highfields, there is no provision for extensive medical care; therefore, when a boy requires hospitalization, it is necessary to transport him to his county hospital or to a private hospital his parents have selected. The fifth sub-category, "Recalled" includes only six boys. In these instances, the judges deemed that another type of disposition would be advisable. In each case, the boys who were recalled were returned home and continued on probation in the community.

The project's experience has been that boys who are unsuitable for residence, and this includes the first three sub-categories, fall into three general groups:

(1) *Devious, hardened delinquents;* i. e., boys who have a deep personal commitment to an antisocial role, and whose rigid, hardened defenses cannot be pierced by the "style of life" of the project, or by the guided group interaction sessions.

(2) *Serious psychiatric problems;* i. e., boys to whom the free, informal rough interplay of the group life at Highfields is too much of a threat.

(3) *Serious runaways;* i. e., boys who leave without any intention of returning or who, after they leave, become involved in other offenses.

It seems that in the flow of life at Highfields, there are times

CHART 3
Boys Unsuitable for Residence
By Month of Separation

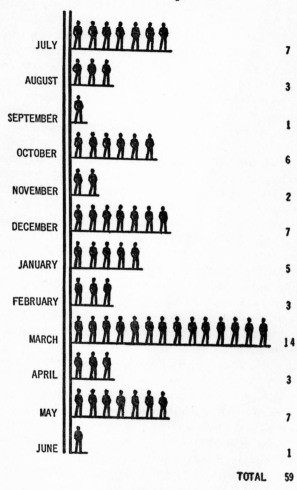

JULY	7
AUGUST	3
SEPTEMBER	1
OCTOBER	6
NOVEMBER	2
DECEMBER	7
JANUARY	5
FEBRUARY	3
MARCH	14
APRIL	3
MAY	7
JUNE	1

TOTAL 59

when the traditions of the project and its "climate" are threatened by a variety of fortuitous circumstances, relating primarily to admission and discharge. On one such occasion, in the month of March, 1952, 11 boys were found to be unsuitable for residence. During this month, the oldest boy in residence had been at the project for only two months. He was a feeble-minded, inadequate, anxious boy, unable to function as an important link in the maintenance of a tradition that had evolved over the years. Only two other boys then in residence had been at the project for more than one month. In neither case were they able to interpret to the new admissions the traditions of the project or make important contributions to the maintenance of these traditions.

At the same time, the courts sent several seriously delinquent boys as well as two or three severely psychologically disturbed boys. Also, the number of boys in residence at the project rose beyond the desirable limits of 16 to 18, to 24 boys. Marked cleavages in groups resulted, and a powerful seventeen-year-old tough hoodlum from the Newark streets, who had recently been dishonorably discharged from the United States Army, sprang into a leadership position. Unable to handle the situation at the project, it was necessary, as a result of a series of antisocial acts committed by the boys in his "gang," to return 11 of them to court. (See Chart 3.)

Also, since the instances of failure tend to cluster at certain times, it seems safe to assume that some boys falling into the category of "Unsuitable for Residence" might have been successfully processed had they been admitted to the project under more auspicious circumstances.

A glance at Chart 4 will show that the boys coming to the project who are unsuitable for residence reveal their deficiencies early, just as Highfields' inability to cope with their problems is exposed soon after their admission. Over three-fourths of these boys remained at Highfields for two months or less. In some instances, they were in residence from a few hours to a few days before running away or being returned to court for another type of disposition. The average length of residence of these boys was three weeks.

Who are the boys that are unsuitable for residence and how do they differ from the boys who are able to complete their period of residence and return to the supervision of the various probation departments? In Table 6, an attempt is made to determine some of these differences by comparing the two groups of residents, in terms of a few selected social factors: place of residence, type of offense, color, age at admission, highest grade completed, and family structure.

CHART 4
Boys Unsuitable for Residence
By Length of Residence
(right-hand numbers indicate percentages)

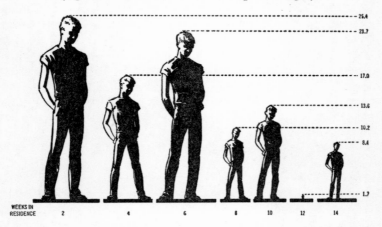

Apparently, the place of residence at the time of admission does not clearly differentiate the two groups of boys who are compared in Table 6. Only slight differences were found between boys who became unsuitable for residence and those who succeeded in returning to probation in the community. However, it is of interest to note that a slightly greater proportion of boys from both rural areas and large urban centers completed their period of retraining than failed to do so, while the trend was in the opposite direction in the case of small town boys. We might assume that a greater proportion of boys from large cities would be found unsuitable than returned to the community, for it is in large urban areas that

TABLE 6

Comparison of Boys Unsuitable for Residence with Boys Returned to Probation at Highfields By Selected Social Characteristics [a]

Social Characteristics [e]	Percent Unsuitable (n = 59)	Percent Ret. to Prob. (n = 240)	Social Characteristics	Percent Unsuitable (n = 59)	Percent Ret. to Prob. (n = 240)
1. *Place of Residence* [b]			4. *Age at Admission*		
Rural	10	14	16 years and under	64	58
Small town	29	23	17 years and older	36	42
Large urban center	61	63			
2. *Type of Offense*			5. *Highest Grade Completed*		
Against property	68	66	8th grade and less	46	40
Against persons	5	17	9–10 grade	51	53
Incorrigible	27	14	11–12 grade	3	7
Others [c]	—	3			
3. *Color*			6. *Family Structure*		
White	88	83	Parents together	31	55
Negro	12	17	One or both deceased	17	22
			Legal break [d]	52	23

[a] Chi-squares were computed for each characteristic and the level of significance ascertained; .05 level of significance was chosen.

[b] Rural—less than 2500; small town—2500–25,000; large urban center—over 25,000.

[c] Narcotics (4); extortion (2); carrying concealed weapons (3).

[d] Boys whose parents were separated, divorced, or deserted, and boys who were adopted.

[e] Only three social characteristics pointed up significant differences; offense, color, and family structure.

the delinquent activities of the gang dominate the street life of the adolescent boy. We might expect then, that these boys are more deeply committed to antisocial attitudes and values than boys who are reared in small towns and rural areas. Since one of the goals of the project is to help the boys change these antisocial attitudes and patterns of conduct, we should expect a greater amount of resistance and conflict among urbanized boys which would lead to their involvement in serious difficulties and subsequently a return to court for another type of disposition, than among boys from small towns and rural areas. While this situation does occur at times, it does not explain the findings in Table 6. One explanation might be that the small-town boys, particularly, are, in many instances, "apron-string" delinquents; boys who are usually labelled as incorrigible or behavior problems because they truant from school habitually, run away from home, create disturbances in the neighborhood or in school, violate traffic ordinances, and are emotionally disturbed as a result of a serious conflict in the family situation. At Highfields, they constitute a small and relatively unorganized group as compared with boys who have delinquent careers that are rooted in the gang. After they arrive at the project these "apron-string" delinquents reveal their anxieties early. Usually they feel that they are "different" from the other boys, whom they regard as "thieves." They conclude, as a result, that they do not "belong" at Highfields. Many of them point out, "I didn't steal anything, I just had a little trouble at home. These boys are thieves. Some of them are hoodlums, they belong here, I don't. I learned my lesson, besides I don't have any problems. I'm not going to get into trouble anymore. I want to go back to court." Other times, they feel threatened by the descriptions of the exploits which the more sophisticated gang delinquents relate over and over again, occasionally in great detail. Also, they are frightened by the argot the other boys employ in communicating with each other. Perhaps the most terrifying experiences occur when they observe or get involved in the extremely hostile, aggressive interplay that takes place between the "hipsters," "hard guys," and "tough guys." In explaining why he had run away, one small town boy said, "I got scared of the boys here. I thought they were crazy the way they fooled around. I just couldn't take it anymore. I never even heard of the things these guys do." In still other instances, boys from small towns are sent to Highfields under the mistaken impression that the guided group interaction sessions are a method of treating psychiatric problems. These boys do not survive at the project, partly because there are no psychiatric facilities and partly because the style of life is too threatening for them. It appears, also, that some small town boys regard themselves as socially "better and wealthier" than the other boys. They regard themselves as members of the middle class and therefore different from the "slum or big city" boys. To many of them, this differentiating characteristic "proves" that they do not belong at Highfields. The implication is, of course, that they belong at home.

By way of contrast, the boys from rural areas are sent to Highfields usually because they have been involved in a series of offenses over a relatively long period of time. They are not just "incorrigible." In a sense, their involvement in these offenses provides them with a link to the other big-city boys. As a result, they find a niche for themselves in the peer-group life around the home. These boys are accepted in the role of "hicks" who, as one "hipster" commented, "You can have a lot of fun with because they don't know anything." This situation probably accounts for the relatively low rate of boys from rural areas among the unsuitables as compared with the number of rural boys who return to probation.

When we examine the types of offenses which the two groups of boys committed, we find that in both instances the overwhelming majority of them were involved in property offenses. In fact, the proportions are almost equal: unsuitable for residence, 68 percent; returned to probation, 66 percent. However, the contrast between them is greater in the case of other types of violations. Very few of the boys who were unsuitable (only 5 percent) committed such offenses against persons as fighting and assault, statutory rape, carnal abuse, and other types of sex offenses; while a significantly greater proportion who completed their residence (17 percent) were involved in similar types of offenses. Another striking difference between these two groups is seen in the "Incorrigible" category, which is a catch-all rubric and includes a variety of offenses such as traffic violations, truancy, ungovernability, and assorted technical violations of the rules of probation. Twenty-seven percent of the boys who did not survive at Highfields were in this same offense category. Apparently, these boys had a more difficult time adjusting to the program than did boys who committed other types of offenses. It is difficult to generalize about the "other offenses," since there are so few cases involved—only 3 percent. However, it should be noted that all of them made a satisfactory adjustment at Highfields.

Turning now to a consideration of the two groups in terms of the racial composition of the boys, we see from the breakdown in Table 6 that there was a significantly greater proportion of white boys who were unsuitable for residence (88 percent) than who completed their stay (83 percent). On the other hand, among the Negroes, a smaller proportion failed to adjust at Highfields (12 percent), than were returned to the supervision of their probation officers (17 percent).[21] In the guided group interaction sessions, where group identification and group solidarity are strong, Negro and white boys learn to accept each other. In fact, this is probably the first opportunity both groups of boys have had to explore problems in concert and to share and understand experiences. Inevitably their participation in these group sessions leads to common membership in peer groups and to joint activities around the house. In one particular group which consisted of two Negroes and seven white boys, there was a great deal of overt hostility by most of the white boys toward the Negroes. This aggression became accentuated when it appeared that the Negroes were making a more satisfactory adjustment than the white boys. There was little interplay between these two groups outside of the group sessions. In fact, when possible, they deliberately

---

[21] Apparently, the chances for survival at Highfields are greater for Negro boys than for white boys. Of the 251 white boys in this study, 51, or 20 percent, failed to adjust satisfactorily to the program, while only 7, or 15 percent, of the 48 Negro boys had a similar experience. (Negro boys constituted 16 percent of the admissions.)

avoided each other around the house and at work, while at other times they engaged in conflicts with each other. Gradually, over a period of several weeks, the members began to develop an understanding of each other's problems. Also, they were almost forced to identify with each other and join together, when the new boys in the other therapy group made disparaging comments about them and indicated that they, the members of the new group, were functioning more smoothly than the old group. One of the new boys pointed out, "Those guys should know better since they've been here longer than we have, but they can't get together, they're always arguing and shouting. They don't even know how to solve problems." Soon a rivalry developed between the two groups. It encouraged the old boys to resolve their differences. One of these white boys decided to move out of his room and into the same room with one of the Negro boys. In explaining this act he stated, "I don't know, I just think Tang (a Negro boy) can help me. We can talk things over at night after we go to bed." A few days later the leader of the white boys' clique went to visit this white boy. To his surprise he observed the Negro boy teaching him how to dance. Shortly thereafter, this leader asked Tang to teach him new dance steps also. In the group meeting when this incident was discussed, the white boy remarked, "It hurt me plenty to ask Tang to teach me a new dance routine. I knew he'd laugh at me and some of the other guys too because I'm not a very good dancer, but I said, 'hell what difference does it make.' He can't be that bad. After all he helps a lot of boys in the meeting."

Also, as a rule Negro boys do not achieve the status of a "duke" at Highfields—that is, a boy who assumes a position of leadership in the peer group life around the house. Consequently, they do not get involved as frequently in situations which would be serious enough to warrant returning them to court for further disposition. On the other hand, some white boys are continually striving to attain high status in the informal group life at the project. In order to secure this status and to maintain it, these boys feel they must engage in conduct which is designed to re-enforce their high status. Consequently, they and their cliques assault other boys, instigate conflicts, challenge the authority of the staff members, and commit acts that other boys are too frightened to get involved in.

While Negro boys do not normally achieve high status as "duke," they do have other channels for securing prestige among their peers. These opportunities assist the Negro boys in accepting the program at Highfields. All boys attain the role of "old boy" merely by virtue of being in residence for a longer period of time than other boys. Boys in this role are regarded usually as "advisors" by the new admissions. There is a degree of prestige associated with this role, sometimes regardless of the kind of adjustment the boy is making. But of even greater significance is the opportunity to achieve high status within the therapy group by "making progress" or "changing." Boys who demonstrate that they have internalized conventional values and attitudes are granted high prestige and social status by the other boys, new and old, especially by members of their own group. If an old boy does not "change," he is not accorded this status; in fact, the chances are that he will lose any status that he had outside the therapy group, especially if he is a clique leader. In a sense then, all boys, Negro and white alike, have available to them a system for achieving high status which is largely independent of the system for assigning status outside of the guided group interaction sessions.

Although it appears that the boys who were unsuitable for residence were younger at the time of admission, in greater proportion (64 percent), than boys who made the grade at Highfields (58 percent), this difference is not statistically significant. Apparently, then, a boy's age at the time of his admission is not a factor in the question of whether or not he will be able to survive at Highfields.

It might be expected that boys who were able to complete their residence at Highfields would have a higher level of educational attainment than boys who did not properly adjust to the program, since in the guided group interaction sessions the ability to verbalize is an aid in communicating ideas and feelings to others. Table 6 reveals that although this expectation tends to be borne out, in that a greater proportion of unsuitable boys than boys who were returned to probation were still in grammar school or had managed to complete the eighth-grade education, these differences were not statistically significant.

When the two groups are compared in terms of the structure of their families, we find that there are significant differences between them. Table 6 shows that the unsuitable boys were part of an intact family situation less frequently than were the boys who survived the Highfields experience. Less than one-third of the unsuitable boys had parents who were living together, while more than half of the boys who completed their residence lived in a similar situation. An interesting finding in the same table is that more than half of the boys who were unsuitable (52 percent) had parents who were involved in court action culminating in a separation, divorce, or adoption of the boy, while less than one quarter of the boys who made a satisfactory adjustment (23 percent) had a similar family experience. Apparently, conflict in the family reduces a boy's chances for survival at Highfields. A non-legal break in the family make-up, such as the demise of one or both parents, however, does not seem to lead to the same disastrous end in Highfields as does a legal rupture. A greater proportion of the boys who survived (22 percent) were in this situation, while only 17 percent of the unsuitable boys had one or two deceased parents.

SUMMARY

In this section we have compared the boys who were unsuitable for residence with those boys who were able to make a sufficiently satisfactory adjustment to permit them to return to the supervision of their respective probation departments in the free community. Six social factors were selected for this purpose. It was found that in some respects these two groups of boys resemble each other: in the place of residence at the time they committed the offense which led to their selection for admission to Highfields, in the ages at the time of their admission, and in the level of educational attainment. However, there were marked differences between these groups in the kinds of offenses they committed, in their racial composition, and in the structure of their families.

The style of life at Highfields is flexible, informal, and dominated by intimate, face-to-face relationships. At the same time it is demanding, intense, and anxiety-provoking. Consequently, when a boy departs from the project, changes take place in the nature and structure of the peer-group relationships. The degree and direction of these changes depends, in large measure, on the conditions surrounding the departure of a boy. When he leaves because he is being returned to court for another disposition, usually a commitment to the state reformatory, or if he runs away, then sudden shifts take place in clique relationships—boys move from one room to another, the discussions in the guided group interaction sessions tend to become hostile and anxiety-laden, and, usually, the group or a portion of it attacks the therapist. When a boy goes home, the shift in the peer groups tend to be less sudden because his departure was expected. These changes do not assume the proportions of a crisis as they do in the former instance.

These group shifts point to the fact that Highfields must be viewed in two quite different lights. On the one hand, as an abstraction, it is a firm, continuing program with a specific philosophy and definite goals. On the other hand, on the concrete level, it is a series of constantly changing groups each with its own structure and problems—a highly unstable culture, held together by fixed principles and aims.

VII

Community Adjustment

THE PROBLEM OF DETERMINING WHETHER OR NOT THE HIGHFIELDS program reforms the boys who are exposed to it is a difficult one to deal with. The same situation exists for any correctional institution which attempts to evaluate the effectiveness of its program in these terms. One of the obstacles here is to find a set of criteria which can be applied to measure the type and degree of reformation which has taken place; in effect, to tell the story of persons who have failed to reform and of those who have changed from delinquency to nondelinquency. Probably one of the most searching and challenging problems in this field is to find a method for demonstrating that reformation, when it does occur, is due to institutional treatment. In other words, do changes in attitudes and conduct occur because of institutional experience and treatment, or in spite of it? Even in the case of the recidivist, the discharged boy who returns to delinquency and eventually is recommitted to a correctional facility, the question arises—did he fail to reform because of the failure of the institution, or was it a result of other factors in the free community which were unrelated to his institutional experience? These problems requiring further study are beyond the scope of this report. However, they should be considered in interpreting the factual data which are presented in this section.

Two commonly employed measures of whether or not reformation has taken place are the recidivist rate and the success rate. These measures are not entirely satisfactory. A boy who is returned to the community and experiences rearrest without conviction, has no visible means of support, associates with other probationers and parolees, gets involved in minor infractions of the rules of probation, but does not get convicted and sentenced— such a boy is regarded as a success according to these measures. But, although they are gross methods, they do shed some light on one important aspect of this problem of determining the kind of adjustment in the free community that has been made by boys who were released from Highfields and returned to the super-

CHART 5
Post-release Adjustment
By Type of Community Adjustment

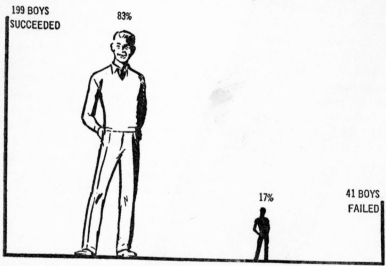

vision of the county probation departments. This information is presented in Chart 5. Here we see that 199, or 83 percent, of all the boys who completed their period of retraining in Highfields made a successful adjustment in the community, while 41, or 17 percent, of the boys failed. A successful adjustment refers to the fact that the boy was still in the free community at the time the study was begun, on June 30, 1955. The kind of adjustment which these boys made while on probation following their release from

Highfields is presented in a later portion of this chapter. Boys who failed were those who committed a new offense or violated the rules of probation and were sentenced to a correctional facility following their release from Highfields.

In the following section, the boys who succeeded and those who failed in the community are compared with each other, in terms of the same social factors which were employed previously. In addition, two other factors are used—namely, length of residence at Highfields and exposure time in the free community. Also, a brief description is presented of the probation officers' ratings of each boy's community adjustment.

An analysis of the place of residence category in Table 7 reveals that boys who resided in large urban centers experienced greater difficulty in making a satisfactory community adjustment following their release from Highfields than did boys who resided in other types of communities. Of the 41 boys who failed, more than three fourths of them lived in large cities, while only 61 percent were successful. It should be noted, however, that these and other differences between the two groups in terms of their place of residence were not statistically significant.

Four types of offenses committed by these boys are also shown in Table 7. Here we find that the differences which are revealed are significant ones. Four fifths of the boys who failed committed property offenses, as compared with less than two thirds of those who were successful. Two other categories, offenses against persons and incorrigible, showed a greater proportion of boys who were successful (19 and 15 percent respectively). In the last category, other types of offenses, the indication is that a greater proportion of the failures (10 percent) were involved in them than were boys who succeeded (3 percent). However, we are dealing with only nine cases here.

Although it is not indicated in this table, it is interesting to note that among the specific offense categories, all of the boys who committed armed robbery (13 cases), 20 out of 21 boys who were involved in fighting and assault, and all of the boys who violated the sex laws (19 cases) were able to survive successfully in the community. On the other hand, the largest proportion of viola-

TABLE 7

Comparison of Successes and Failures by Selected Social Characteristics [a]

Social Characteristics	Percent Successes (n = 199)	Percent Failures (n = 41)	Social Characteristics	Percent Successes (n = 199)	Percent Failures (n = 41)
1. *Place of Residence* [b]			4. *Age at Admission*		
Rural	14	14	16 years and under	64	34
Small town	25	10	17 years and older	40	66
Large urban centers	61	76			
2. *Type of Offense*			5. *Highest Grade Completed*		
Against property	63	80	8th grade and less	40	44
Against persons	19	3	9–10 grade	53	54
Incorrigible	15	7	11–12 grade	7	2
Others	3 [c]	10 [d]			
3. *Color* [e]			6. *Family Structure*		
White	85	73	Parents together	55	56
Negro	15	27	One or both deceased	23	15
			Legal break [f]	22	29

[a] Chi-squares were computed for each characteristic and the level of significance ascertained; .05 level of significance was chosen.

[b] Rural—less than 2500; small town—2500–25,000; large urban center—over 25,000.

[c] Extortion (4); carrying concealed weapons (2); narcotics (1).

[d] Narcotics (3), carrying concealed weapons (1)

[e] Significant differences were found in case of only two social characteristics: type of offense and color.

[f] Boys whose parents were separated, divorced, and boys who were adopted.

tions were committed by boys whose original offense was larceny, especially auto larceny.

Although Negro boys are able to make a more satisfactory adjustment during their residence at Highfields than white boys (cf. Table 6), they do not seem to carry over into the community this same pattern of adjustment. Table 7 shows that boys who were successful were white significantly more often (85 percent) than boys who failed (73 percent). On the other hand, fewer of the boys who succeeded were Negroes (15 percent) than boys who were convicted of another offense and sentenced to another correctional facility (27 percent).[22]

The indications from the age at admission category are that successful boys were younger more frequently than the boys who failed. However, the differences that do exist are not important ones.

As in the previous section (cf. Table 6), where it was seen that there was no significant association between level of educational attainment and type of adjustment at Highfields, so in Table 7 we find again that no significant differences exist between level of scholastic achievement and failure or success in the free community. Almost equal proportions of boys who made a satisfactory community adjustment (40 percent) and boys who failed to do so (44 percent) obtained an eighth grade diploma or ended their formal education while still in grammar school. The same situation exists for boys who completed the 9th and 10th grades (successful—53 percent, failed—54 percent). A slightly higher proportion of successes (7 percent), than failures (2 percent) completed the 11th and 12th grades.

The findings in the family structure category are somewhat surprising. It would appear that Highfields "graduates" would have a more favorable opportunity to survive in the free community if they came from homes that were parentally intact than from broken homes. The unity represented by an intact home would be expected to provide a stabilizing and controlling influence on these boys, while the absence of one or both parents in

---

[22] It should be noted also, that the failure rate for white boys alone was .15 while the failure rate for Negroes alone was almost twice as high, .27.

the home would tend to mitigate this influence so that boys from these homes would be expected to have higher failure rates than boys who completed their period of residence. An equal proportion of boys who were successful and boys who failed had parents who were alive and in the same home. Although there were some differences between successes and failures when they were compared in terms of type of a break in the family structure, the differences were not statistically significant. A greater incidence of parents who were deceased were found among the successes (23 percent) than among the failures (15 percent). The trend was in the opposite direction when a legal break in the family structure such as divorce or desertion occurred, for here the successes experienced a lower proportion (22 percent) than the failures (29 percent). Of course, here we are dealing only with the external aspect of the family structure. The nature and quality of the interpersonal relationships in the family may have a more marked effect on these boys than is revealed here.

There does not seem to be any significant difference between the two groups of boys in terms of the length of time they spent in residence at Highfields. Of course, not all boys are able to make gains at the same pace, nor is there a uniform, specific goal set for all boys. Moreover, the "social climate" at the house and the extent to which each therapy group is able to develop into a cohesive unit are other factors which play important roles in the length of time each boy spends at Highfields. Once a boy returns to his community, other factors are called into play which vary in the influence they exert on his adjustment. However, when this particular factor, length of residence at the project, is investigated, we find that it is not significantly associated with failure or success at home. The boys who survived in the community following their discharge from Highfields were in residence for three months or less more frequently (16 percent) than boys who failed in the community (7 percent). However, a smaller proportion of the boys who succeeded spent four months or more in residence (84 percent) than the boys who failed (93 percent). The average length of residence of boys who succeeded and those who failed was the same in each case, 15 weeks.

Experience with released offenders and with probationers indicates that the period immediately following their release from a correctional institution or placement on probation is a crucial one, for it is during this time that failure rates are highest. Highfields graduates are not exceptions in this case, for, as Chart 6 reveals, over half of the failures (56 percent) occurred before the end of the first year of post-Highfields experience. Only 20 percent of the successes were in the community for the same length

CHART 6
Post-release Adjustment
By Exposure Time Periods
(numbers indicate percentages)

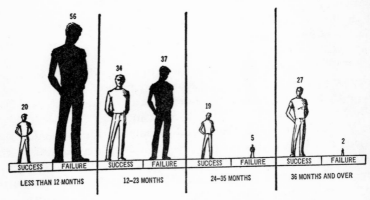

| SUCCESS | FAILURE | SUCCESS | FAILURE | SUCCESS | FAILURE | SUCCESS | FAILURE |
| LESS THAN 12 MONTHS | | 12–23 MONTHS | | 24–35 MONTHS | | 36 MONTHS AND OVER | |

of time. Almost all of the remainder of the failures (37 percent) occurred during the second year of post-release exposure. Over one third of the successful boys (34 percent) were still in the community during the same time period. In other words, almost all of the boys failed during the first two years after they returned to their homes, while only slightly more than half of the successes had been exposed to the free community for a similar period. It should be noted, too, that more than one fourth of the successes had left Highfields three or more years previously, while only 2 percent of the failures had been home for such a relatively long period of time. All of the differences in Chart 6 were found to be statistically significant.

A picture of the boys' adjustment in the community made by the probation officers who supervised them is presented in Chart 7. A schedule was sent to the county probation department requesting a rating from the officers on five aspects of community adjustment as follows: relationship with the probation officer, relationships with the family, the boy's attitude toward himself, work adjustment and overall adjustment on probation. All of the schedules were completed and returned.

In this section the most favorable results were found in the data

CHART 7

Probation Officers' Evaluation of Five Phases of Community Adjustment of 199 Successes

(numbers indicate percentages)

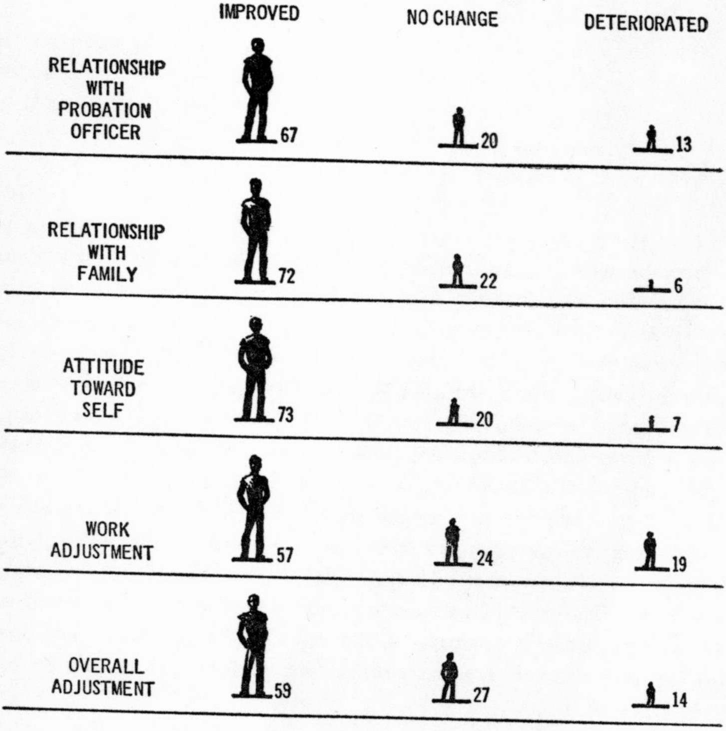

	IMPROVED	NO CHANGE	DETERIORATED
RELATIONSHIP WITH PROBATION OFFICER	67	20	13
RELATIONSHIP WITH FAMILY	72	22	6
ATTITUDE TOWARD SELF	73	20	7
WORK ADJUSTMENT	57	24	19
OVERALL ADJUSTMENT	59	27	14

dealing with the boys' attitudes toward themselves, an area of special emphasis during their stay at Highfields. Almost three fourths of the boys showed some improvement here. On the other hand, that phase of community adjustment concerning work showed the least improvement. This is not surprising, since very few of the boys had any kind of work experience prior to their admission. Also, it is the area in which they had a great deal of difficulty adjusting to while in residence. Even so, more than half of the boys were reported as having achieved a definite change in their work habits. All in all, the probation officers reported that, in their judgment, the majority of the boys showed improvement in all phases of their adjustment after release from Highfields.

SUMMARY

The foregoing analysis has shown that there are some significant differences between the boys who succeeded in the community and those who failed. It is clear that failures were involved in property offenses in greater degree than in any other type of violations as compared with the successes. Moreover, Negro boys failed in greater proportion than white boys, although, at Highfields, Negroes made a more satisfactory adjustment. Another difference between the successes and the failures was in the exposure time in the free community. As expected, the failures spent much less time in the community following their release from Highfields than the boys who succeeded.

Some similarities were also found between the two groups. Although boys who failed tended to have urban backgrounds in greater proportion than boys who made a successful community adjustment, the difference was not significant. In the case of the factor of age at time of admission, while the incidence of success was greater among younger boys than older ones, again the difference was not important. It was found, too, that level of educational attainment was not associated with successful adjustment in the community. Approximately equal proportions of successes and failures were in grade school at the time of admission or had managed to graduate from the eighth grade. A similar situation existed for boys who were in high school. The two groups were alike as regards the structure of their families. While this factor seemed to play a significant role in the type of adjustment that was made at Highfields, it was not important in differentiating boys who made a successful adjustment in the community from those who did not. Apparently, other factors in the community had a greater impact on the boys after their release than the external family structure. Also, there were no significant differences between the successes and failures in the length of time they spent at Highfields, although the former group tended to spend less time in residence than the latter group.

Moreover, we tried to find out how the probation officers who supervised the boys after their release from Highfields rated them in five important areas of community adjustment. Apparently the greatest improvement was reported in each boy's attitude toward himself and the least change in the area of work adjustment. A very high proportion of boys were rated as having made improvements in their interpersonal relationships, specifically with their probation officers and with the members of the boys' families. Too, the probation officers felt that more than half of the boys made a positive change in their overall adjustment.

No doubt there are other factors which have not been considered in this section which may be more crucial in distinguishing the successes from the failures, such as the nature of the interpersonal relationships in the family, the frequency and intensity of associations with delinquent peer groups, conceptions of themselves, and attitudes toward conventional standards and others. We have not attempted to present an exhaustive analysis of this problem; our aim has been only to suggest what influence some of the factors had in the type of community adjustment made by the boys who were released from Highfields following the completion of a period of retraining.

VIII

Results of a Projective Test[*]

IN CONSIDERING WHETHER THE HIGHFIELDS TYPE OF PROGRAM IS MORE or less effective than conventional reformatory routines one may, if he chooses, base his conclusions solely on the relative costs and recidivist rates at Highfields and its alternatives. However, if this were done, the only truly valid conclusion which could be drawn is whether or not Highfields, on the basis of these data alone, justified its existence. One still would not know in what direction the superiority lay; how the conventional reformatory program might be altered to compete with Highfields if the latter has a better record; how Highfields itself might be improved; nor even how the experience could be duplicated in another "Highfields" were that course deemed wise. To answer these questions, one must have some notion about the way in which Highfields affected the personality of the delinquent in contrast to the conventional reformatory. One should know also how the observed differences are related to treatment methods on the one hand and to the probability of recurrence of antisocial behavior on the other.

The usual approach to these questions is to arrange for careful psychiatric and psychological examination on admission to and release from the institutions under comparison. Such a procedure was considered in this study but was impractical for several reasons. Administrative procedures simply would not permit all the young men at Highfields and at a conventional reformatory to go through an adequate examining routine. The amount of pro-

[*] The material contained in this chapter was supported by the Vincent Astor Foundation and prepared by the late Dr. Quinter Holsopple, member of the Scientific Advisory Committee of the Foundation.

fessional service required was not available within the existing or readily procurable limits of psychiatric and psychological staff. Perfunctory examinations might be actually misleading. Furthermore, many authorities would question the financial wisdom of launching an expensive inquiry into the nature of the superiority of Highfields treatment before there was any real assurance of its value in the simple respect of reducing recidivism.

Fortunately, we were not wholly without resources. The Miale-Holsopple Sentence Completion [23] Technique provided useful data, well within the resources of the project, which threw some light on the personality changes occurring during the course of treatment at a conventional reformatory and at Highfields. Ordinarily this instrument is used in conjunction with interviews, tests, social history, and related technical and professional data in arriving at judgments about personality. However, it can also be used coordinately with such data and independently of them. Under such circumstances it has shown considerable value. No matter how unbiased the psychiatrist or psychologist may try to be, he cannot help reacting during an examination to what he knows and feels about the situation from which his subject comes. With the sentence completion he is not influenced by these factors. Thus, we can confirm the inferences from the sentence completion by their congruence with staff observations and with the more objective circumstances of recidivism. This we did by submitting the sentence completion of 26 conventional reformatory and 25 Highfields boys, before and after treatment, to scrutiny by two psychologists. One, Mr. Richard Benjamin, a competent analyst of sentence completions, knew nothing of the nature of the project, the program at a conventional reformatory or Highfields, and nothing about the background or behavior of the boys. The other was J. Q. Holsopple who, with Mrs. F. Miale, designed the technique. Their conclusions were for the most part identical, and at no point in disagreement.

It must be noted that the sentence completion technique is not

---

[23] J. Q. Holsopple and F. R. Miale, *Sentence Completion, A Projective Technique for the Study of Personality.* Charles C. Thomas: Springfield, 1954, pp. xiii, 7, 177.

merely a simple paper and pencil "test" which can be readily
"scored" and "interpreted" mechanically by use of a key. It is a
sensitive, projective method requiring a high degree of skill on
the part of the examiner. It has demonstrated its utility in such
diverse situations as a study of effects of prefrontal lobotomy [24]
and in the identification of those persons failing to make adequate adjustment in overseas governmental assignments.[25] Experience with the Highfields project adds to our confidence in
the technique and throws light on the changes occurring in our
delinquent subjects.

We may now turn to some tentative conclusions which may be
justified by the projective material.

(1) The two groups are not wholly indistinguishable at the
time of admission, but they resemble each other more than either
group resembles a noninstitutional, nondelinquent group of its
age—for example, a group of newly inducted enlisted young men
in the Armed Forces—with which we could make a comparison.
The Highfields boys on admission are a little brighter, a little
less bitter, hostile, and suspicious than the conventional reformatory group. These initial differences, however, are small as compared with the differences in the amount and direction of changes
which appear after treatment.

(2) Generalization for either group must always be drawn with
the stipulation that there are exceptions. For example, a few of
the conventional reformatory boys seemed to move in the favorable direction which appeared to be more characteristic of the
Highfields group. But on the whole there seems little probability
that the *group* differences are accidental.

(3) The Highfields boys moved in the direction of frankness,

---

[24] R. L. Jenkins and J. Q. Holsopple, "Criteria and Experimental Design for
Evaluating Results of Lobotomy," *Proc. of Assn. for Research in Nervous
and Mental Disease*. William and Wilkins: Baltimore, 1953, pp. 319–327; R. L.
Jenkins, J. Q. Holsopple, and M. L. Lorr, "Effects of Prefrontal Lobotomy
on Patients with Severe Chronic Schizophrenia," Amer. J. Psychiat., 3, 84–90,
1954.
[25] S. Kavruck, "The Sentence Completion Technique as a Means of Predicting
the Personality Adjustment of Federal Employees Serving Overseas." Doctoral
dissertation, George Washington University, 1954.

expressiveness, and recognition of social values (not always acceptance, but at least awareness). The conventional reformatory boys in contrast became more guarded, covered their thoughts under clichés (if indeed they did not move toward thinking in clichés), and avoided coming to grips with issues of importance—social or personal.

(4) Both groups on admission would have to be characterized as "unhappy." But whereas the conventional reformatory group developed quite uniformly a bleaker, darker, and more depressed outlook, the Highfields group showed a generally positive and more varied, more realistic outlook. To be sure, this very realism invited some depression and considerable anxiety because they were leaving the institution to face genuine problems—and they knew it. Both the depression and anxiety had a quality of appropriateness which was lacking in the conventional reformatory records.

Both groups at the outset handled their problems of dealing with authority badly. They felt weak and insecure, reacted petulantly and rebelliously, and indulged in fantasy. The conventional reformatory boys tended to develop withdrawal, weak acceptance of authority, a pessimistic fatalism, and techniques of saying the "right words." The Highfields group could hardly be said to have achieved real maturity, or full ability to exercise or surrender to authority as might be appropriate, but they were moving in that direction. To be sure, they had anxiety about it and found the outlook somewhat depressing, but they could see the future as both good and bad. They could begin to manage conflict without suppressing one aspect of reality or its conflicting opposite.

If we reduce the observed changes to a somewhat oversimplified statement, it might be that the Highfields boys had begun to gain, while the conventional reformatory boys had lost, some of their initially too limited *self-respect*. Should this statement be true, it would go a long distance toward explaining the striking advantage of Highfields in dealing with the Negro delinquent.

Whatever causal relation there may be between membership in a persecuted, repressed minority group and the fact of delin-

quency should operate to reduce that delinquency when a successful effort is made to increase self-respect. What seems to be true
is that Highfields is good for the white delinquent, but even
better for the Negro.

The pressures and forces controlling the conventional reformatory group prior to admission were perceived by the boys as
hostile and repressive. The life in the conventional reformatory
accentuates that perception. For Highfields, the freedom of
movement and expression, the encouragement by the administration to experiment with varied behavior patterns, and the opportunity to exchange opinions and views clearly shifted the
character of perceived pressure from "hostility" and "repression"
toward what might properly be termed as "challenge."

There is no reason to suppose that the primary goals or basic
drives of either group were substantially changed. With the conventional reformatory group on the one hand, the goals remained
distorted or unclear, the drives unrecognized or unaccepted. In
contrast, among the Highfields group, there was movement toward a clearer view of primary goals and substantially increased
acceptance of primary drives.

The changes imputed to both the Highfields boys and the conventional reformatory group seemed clear in the sample studied.
Moreover they are congruent with what we know about reformatory life in general and with the letters written by the Highfields
boys. Nevertheless we cannot at this point wholly exclude the
possibility that these changes in this particular group are the
result of the happy coincidence of a new and surprising method
of treatment, applied by an ingenious, sympathetic, industrious
management, to a group of delinquents whose capacity for rehabilitation was inherently high.

To concede that such a possibility exists by no means dimin-
ishes the impressiveness of the Highfields experiment. It simply
imposes a heavy social obligation to discover whether Highfields
is in fact a fortunate accident—and if it is that, to discover the
conditions under which it can be depended on to recur.

IX

The Boys' Own Story

WHEN A BOY IS NOTIFIED OF HIS PENDING RELEASE, USUALLY, ONE OR two days beforehand, he is given the opportunity to describe his experiences at Highfields as well as anything else he may wish. The overwhelming majority of the boys do so, and on the morning of their departure they turn in their "Own Story." In a sense, these stories provide another opportunity to evaluate the program.

Highfields, Hopewell, New Jersey

Report of Steve

Well, Mr. M——, by the time you read this I'll be on my way home. I guess the best way for me to start is to go back to when I first started stealing. I was about 8 years old at the time. I had just moved to I—— after the lady I lived with died. I didn't like the place where I was living at but I never stayed there much. I used to go down to the five and tens and steal candy, locks and other articles. Half of which I could never use, then I started to steal regular day after day. I then moved to live with another lady in I——. I was about 10 years old at the time. There was two other boys there and they were brothers. We got along good and soon discovered that we all were crooks. So we started to steal little things. This kept up for awhile and then one day one boy came to us and told us about a food market near our house which had a broken cash register. So each day we went and stood with our backs to the register, reached up behind us, pulled out the drawer and lifted some bills out. This was going on a month until one day the cops picked us up and put us in parental school. The other two boys were sent to Jamesburg and I went to the Protectory. I spent 2½ years there and finally after I graduated

I was let go home. I went to live with my stepmother and father. I was getting along fairly well until the summer. My father then sent me away to camp for the summer. But after 6 weeks I wanted to go home but he told me that he had payed for 9 weeks, so I thought that I better stay. About a week later I stole a watch, was caught and sent home. When I arrived my father said that he was putting me in a home and he decided to put me back in the Protectory. I spent about a year there and was thrown out for getting into and causing too much trouble. When I left I went to live in H—— and I liked it a lot. I made a lot of new friends and was getting along good until I got into some trouble in school and was thrown out. I then started to work as an errand boy down N—— and in February (1950) I went to live in P——. I then started to hang around with this boy I knew in the Protectory. One day he told me that D—— was back from Jamesburg, so we went up to see him. I then started to hang around with him. After a few weeks we started to steal. Every day we used to meet, go to the movies and then go out at night and look for houses to break into. Except for the nights I went to see my girl. Even some nights when I went to see her, D—— used to come up and meet me and I'd leave early to go pull some job. We were doing this about a month and then one day we met C——. D—— knew him from Jamesburg. So we teamed up and C—— decided that we should steal a car and pull some jobs. We did and then went down the shore where we were caught the following day. We were sent back to N—— and then went to court. Thats where I first met Mr. M—— and Highfields came into my life.

When I first arrived at Highfields Mr. M—— told me about the rules and privileges and I was there a day or two. I felt, well, this place is pretty soft. I'll be good and get out as soon as I can. I figured I'd say the right things so M—— would think I was making progress and figuring out my problems. But after a while I found out it wasn't that easy and M—— wasn't so crazy after all. Up until a few weeks ago I didn't even think I had anything to figure out, that M—— was just trying to put ideas in my head. But then I started to think about them and discovered everything that he said and told me seemed to fit together and was quite sensible. The climax which really made me believe in Mr. M—— and Highfields was when I had a talk with him about my father wanting me to go into the Navy. Everything came out and made things clear in my mind. I really, honestly and truly, believe that my main problem was my relations with my father and now I feel that I understand him more and he understands me. I feel that when I leave here Sunday my relations with my father will be much better and understanding than when I first arrived at Highfields. I feel that Highfields has really been helpful to me and has given me an experience and a lesson that I shall never forget and I feel that it has really helped me, and I will find out whether or not it has when I go home and face the problem that I had when I came here.

In the future I'm going to try to be more independent and express my feelings towards him (my father) over certain things. And another thing I'm going to hang around with decent people.

Report of Pete

My Past—

Dec. 6, 1950

I'm going to try to explain and be honest about my past, my stay at Highfields and my future plans.

I would rather start about myself from ten years on. I was a model type boy, I was happy and I felt I had everything to live for. I was very close to my mother and family. Very close to my mother.

I never wanted to let my mother down. Then when I was twelve years old my mother passes away. I took it very hard, but because I was young at the time it didn't take me long to get over it. Since I was a little boy my main ambition was to be very famous. I wanted to be a big-shot and there is still that feeling inside of me today.

I was brought up in a pretty tough Italian section of N——. I was always looking for excitement. I used to be the one with all the nerve.

I learned things pretty fast, but the time I was 14 years old I knew what was happening. From 12 years to 14—these two years were really the foundation of what really started me. I started to act different in the 7th grade in grammar school. When I reached 8th I was well on my way. I started to be indifferent to the Sisters and other people. I used to enjoy doing wrong to saying things wrong to the Sisters in class, and then they would lecture to me. That made me feel as if I was the big-shot, the important guy. I acquired a pretty good reputation, I was the tough little guy.

Everybody seemed to like me. I required the reputation as a crazy guy with a knife when I was young. I broke out of that habit of being crazy with a knife or trying to act tough. I wasn't tough at all. Half the time I was scared to fight, but because inside of me would say what would others think of you. So I had to live up to what people said about me. I used to enjoy people feeling sorry for me. It made me feel so much better. Then when I started High School I was determined to go through and do well. I done well for two years. But when I was in my second year, my sister got married and I had to move with her to I—— about seven miles out of the section I live. I didn't want to go then, because I thought they were all squares and I wouldn't like it. I wouldn't be able to see the things they were doing. I didn't like my brother-in-law. To me he was sneaky and so many other things. I still feel the same way, and I'll always feel the same way about him. I moved there in May when I was 15. I had gotten a job before I moved up there. I was working for my sister whose husband owned a Confectionery store. My hours were from 6 to 10 and on Saturdays to 11 and 12. It was a very dull life and I really didn't like it, but I stuck it out for about 16 months. I never took any money from the store until I was there over a year. I was still attending school and I had started my third year at High School in N——.

I started to play hookey almost 2 to 3 times a week, I was just disgusted. During this time I started to rob money from the register. I averaged $10 to $15 almost every week until I was fired.

I wasn't fired because I was caught but because things got so bad that I never went to work, I used to take a lot of days off.

I couldn't see myself working on hot summer nights when everybody was enjoying themselves but me. I had money but I was never happy. I flunked out my first six months in my third year of high school.

I then started I—— High School, I got transferred. My people thought that would be the best for me. I attended for two months and I quit because my grades weren't very good. I still used to play hookey. I told the principal if it would be alright to start all over in September. He said it was alright, and this was in April when I quit. That summer I got fired from work. I felt lost at first but I got over it. I started to stay out late at night, sometimes I wouldn't go home for two or three days. I would always lie to my sisters and Father about where I was. I was always drunk, yes Mr. M——, I never really told you but I was a lush. It really started last Summer when I just turned 17. I used to buy wine every night, real cheap wine for 39¢ and get drunk. I used to hang around the Penn. Station and look around for easy money. Yes, I done a lot of crooked things before I held up the diner. I stole before and robbed people. Nothing serious enough for the police to get worked up about. It was always little things. I went back to school in Sept. last. My drinking was still going strong. I also used to take benny, thats benderizine. If a could have gotten dope I probably would have taken it. But I was satisfied at just getting high. I used to go to a lot of dances last winter and I was always high at almost every one of them. I was with a gang and we were always getting enough fights. I probably got into just as much gang fights as Larry. I was a zoot suit kid too. I was always the hep kid who knew the ropes. I used to give all the girls a line, I'd enjoy letting a girl fall for me, and then I would make myself not bother with them after I knew I had them where I wanted them. To me they were all a bunch of sluts.

I tried to work every girl that I went out with. If I could not beat them for their money I tried to lay them. I never had much trouble getting a girl. But when I did, I felt like hell because they didn't fall for me. I thought it was impossible. Then last winter my big-shot ideas really started to work on me. I was disgusted at home with myself and other things. Mostly because I didn't feel like I used to when I was a little boy of 12 years old.

I was always feeling sorry for myself. I'd lay in bed every night and think of myself as a big gangster with all the money and a lot of respect from everybody. I done it every night and I do it here now, but not so much as before.

I just wanted to do something outstanding. So, all last winter I wanted to pull a job. I trust you more now than I ever did because of the talk we had Dec. 10th. During last winter and Spring and part of the Summer I done many crooked things.

I told you all of the things I did, and I was pretty lucky I usually always got away with it. Well, I finally found the right guys to do the job, so I pulled my holdup. I held the gun because it made me feel good and that was the main guy and they had to respect me. I got away with the job we pulled. But I had a holdup planned that didn't work, before I pulled this holdup. I wanted to graduate, but then I met my girl and I started to go steady. My friends would come around and ask me to meet them, so we could pull another job. But I never went. I wanted something real big to do, probably thats the reason why I didn't go and because of my girl. I was offered a good deal once to pull an $8,000 holdup, but I refused. I don't know if I was scared, or maybe I wanted to get rid of my aggression another way.

Then after a few weeks after the holdup my friend was picked up and he implicated me and three other guys. There is probably lots more I could say, but I think this is sufficient or maybe I'm still a little suspicious of you.

My Stay at High Fields—Dec. 20, 1955

Wel, tomorrow I'm going home, so I'm going to try to explain my stay at High Fields.

When I first came here, I still had intentions of pulling more jobs when I was released.

To me this place was a gig, real easy to do four months and that you and High Fields was a bunch of bull. I figured I do the right things and put on a good front for four months. Try and do some smooth talking to you and everybody connected with High Fields.

So many times I felt like telling you to go and f—— yourself. I'm being real honest now of what I wanted to say to you. I felt like telling you that today Dec. 20th when I didn't go with M. L——. But I'm over it now. I learned a lot of things about myself, that I didn't want to know about or hear them. I learned things that I didn't know about myself. I feel much better inside now, than I ever did before. Now, this place to me isn't bull, it took me quite a long time to figure it out but I think I got most of it. I was always getting disappointed, and that made me hate you all the more. Last Sunday the 17th to me you were the rottenest bastard on the earth, but now you are alright. I could say so much more, but I think this is all I want to say truthfully.

I still can't say for sure I won't get into anymore trouble because of you and Highfields. All I got to do now, is to go out there and face things in a different way. As you told me, if I get time I'll be doing it, not you, and I don't want to do time.

All I could say more, is that I wish this plan is a success, and I think it will. What I think though is that the boys should realize it that they are getting a good break and not take everything as a joke. Maybe I'm just saying these things, because it is all over with, but I find out for sure when I'm out in the streets again.

My Future, Dec. 20th

Well, I can't say I'll never get into anymore trouble, and that I'll be an angel forever. I got a fairly good idea of the situation I was in before. All I got to do now, is that when the same situation arises again, notice it and take it and take it different from that I was taking it. I haven't changed or things on the outside haven't changed. They'll be the same things as before. I'll still get mad, and probably want to make easy money. I still go on hating the same people. But I got to let some of my aggression out and not let it out in a harmful way.

I'm going back to school, and after I'm through with school about a year after I'm getting married. Only the future will answer my question of staying out of trouble. Everybody leaves with good intentions, but I'll need more than that. I like to work, so I don't think I'll have any trouble in that field.

Report of Bob

To whom it may concern:

During my stay at Highfields which lasted three and one-half months I learned many things which I didn't even think of before coming here. It didn't take me long to get used to the place even though in the beginning I resented being sent here. To me this was my idea of a raw deal. If I was to be sent away for the first thing I ever did wrong I was going to show the judge and every body else that they were wrong. After being here about three weeks however, I had time enough to think things over and decided that since I was going to have to have to stay here for awhile I might as well try and help myself. Nobody cared if I didn't want to help myself by being stubborn so I figured it was time I wised up. And that was what I did—wise up.

Before coming here I didn't care about my family, school, work, or just about anything else that was important. Now I have respect for my mother who has stuck by me through all the trouble and heartache I have caused her. I can now see the importance of a high school education, which I thought was just something required by the state. I had the same attitude towards every job I ever had. Whether it was being a delivery boy or working on a construction job. To me it was always the same. Work for awhile until I had saved some money and then quit the job to go out and spend the money carelessly. Now I know the importance of holding a steady job and what leaving it may have on my future.

One of the big problems I had was my disrespect for authority which I have learned to overcome. I have also learned to respect people regardless of race, creed, or color.

In closing I would like to say that if there were more places like Highfields, instead of X—— or Y——, there wouldn't be as many boys going wrong after coming out of an institution.

Report of Chuck

"The Story of My Life"

I was born in P——, New Jersey. I lived in P—— until I was about 3 years old and I moved to my uncle's ranch in Texas. I lived there until I was 9 years old and moved back East to C——, New Jersey where I am living now. I was always getting into trouble in school and ever since I started and I never did like school too much. In fact I was kicked out of every school I went to.

My trouble really started when I entered my Freshman year of High School, and I met a boy who taught me how to steal cars. At first I didn't pay any attention to him but after awhile curiosity got me and I decided to find out for my self what it was like. At first I didn't get caught and I kept on doing it. The first time I got caught I was let go, so I believed I could keep on doing it without getting in trouble. But I was mistaken, the second time I was caught, the judge sent me away for a year, when I got out I thought I had learned my lesson, but I learned different later on. After I turned seventeen I asked my probation officer if I could have my licence but he said no.

I was pretty mad and I decided that I was going to drive whether my probation officer said no or not. Therefore I stole another car and I got caught and when I went to court, the judge sent me to Highfields.

At Highfields, I learned alot as to how to avoid trouble and how to take orders from my elders and also how to control my moodiness. And as one boy said, I learned how to laugh. And now that I am about to leave Highfields I hope to start anew and try to make something of my self besides a hoodlum.

✕   *Report of George*

"The Career of G—— B—— at Highfields"

Part One:

My troubles started on the outside with a group of older boys I hung around with. They were more advanced in the knowledge of girls, drinking and stealing and that made me feel through them as being an adult. So, I wanted to grow up in my mind to be one of them. I tried but they would not accept me. I guess one reason was I didn't look old enough to pass for a fellow eighteen, so I could drink in a tavern over in New York. I knew the only time they accepted me was when I had some money. As far as the money problem was concerned I earned it playing a queer, which got me started on my way, when I didn't have any money I made it a habit to go to this queer's house to receive it from him in return for his favor.

Part two:

Being the older group wouldn't let me hang around with them I then went and made my new friends, who I was willing to use to reach my goal. I then got mixed up in a rape charge, went to court and was put on probation. I then continued to get into trouble. Broke probation by running away with another boy I was trying to use. Was then returned to court for violation of probation. Again was released in my brother's hand. I couldn't get along with my sister-in-law so I got in trouble with her and made her despise me. I felt I wasn't wanted so I went ahead in my action to get revenge for the way she was treating me by telling everything I knew about her. I then made hate in my family so my brother felt the best thing for me was to go back to court.

Part three:

I was then sent to Highfields where I thought I was going to have a pick nick. At first at Highfields when I found out I was not on no pick nick and that the boys didn't acept me again as a grown up I started feeling sorry for my self. I didn't do very much to help myself at Highfields. They felt maybe a furlough would help me. It did. I was able to learn to look toward the future, help myself, stand for my rights, respect adults, work, learn to say no to trouble instead of yes, learn how to keep friends and the way most of the boys didn't like me, also, I learned how to understand people, which is the reason I learned to help the boys in the meeting. Also, to think before I do something wrong again.

Part four:

I was able to understand why I made my mistakes and the reasons why I do them. I found out I was not interested in those things anymore.

Well I could keep writing all week on the things I did in Highfields but I feel I covered most of the things that will help me on the outside.

X

A Comparison of Highfields and Reformatory Graduates*

It is commonplace in correctional work to set up a new program or a new institution with the hope that the "good intentions" which led to its establishment will suffice to maintain it through the years. Since little or no effort is made to evaluate these programs, in time they become just another piece in the correctional puzzle that is penology in the United States. Largely to offset this possibility, an evaluation program was built into the Highfields program. The research reported in this chapter is one effort to determine its effectiveness.

A. RESEARCH DESIGN

1. *Objectives:* To compare the Highfields program with conventional management for effects upon youthful offenders.

2. *Context:* Judges are frequently confronted with youthful offenders whom they are very hesitant to commit to a conventional reformatory school. Yet they are reluctant to return some of these delinquents to the community on probation status because they fear that the family and community situation will be further demoralizing and possibly the risks of recidivism are too great. The Highfields project was created as a third alternative for the management of offenders in this situation.

* This study was under the supervision of Dr. Rupert Hester, Mr. Albert Elias, and Dr. Lloyd McCorkle. The field investigator was Mr. Horace Voltz, Jr. The study was made possible by a grant from the Astor Foundation.

3. *Subjects and Controls:* It appears reasonable to assume that had not the Highfields project been created some of the delinquents entering the project would have been committed to Annandale Farms Reformatory. Others, perhaps, would have been placed upon probation status. An adequate appraisal of the project, therefore, should include comparison between:

a. Highfields delinquents and delinquents committed to Annandale Farms.

b. Highfields delinquents and delinquents placed on probation status.

This study is only concerned with (a).

4. *Approach:* This report was prepared as part of a proposed study of relatively long-range effects on the Highfields program to be based primarily upon (a) available records held by the State of New Jersey and (b) brief follow-up contacts concerning each offender.

5. *Criteria:* Broadly speaking, two criteria of rehabilitation appear feasible: recidivism rates and adjustment following release from respective facilities.

a. Recidivism: The most simple index is simply recidivism rate per exposure. Some requirement of this index appears both feasible and warranted. Specifically we might consider

1) Recidivism rate per exposure time.

2) Number of offenses before next commitment (or before any commitment for offenders initially placed upon probation). This index will be of value only if there are delinquents appearing before the courts and placed upon probation after release from a correctional institution (or before any commitment in a possible group initially placed upon probation).

3) Character of offenses (legal terminology).

b. Adjustment: In one sense recidivism is a basic criterion; yet it may be unfair to Highfields. This possibility becomes evident if we assume that for some offenders brought to the courts recidivism is unlikely regardless of court action (within the usual alternatives). It is possible, for example, to suppose that in some cases delinquent behavior in a sense is circumstantial, depending upon the situation and a personal and social crisis with which the youth is confronted. In such cases the wisdom of court action and institutional management must be evaluated in terms of its effects upon the ability of the youth to shape his destiny in an unfavorable situation, that is, in terms of effects upon his self-respect and personal integrity. Such, clearly, was a basic concept in forming the Highfields program. It would not be feasible, and perhaps it would be futile, to try to explore the effects of Highfields upon the personal life of its discharges in any detailed way. Nevertheless, if the impact of the institution were profound, widespread, and lasting, it should be reflected in the indices below:

1) Work record since discharge: number of jobs (frequency of job changes), extent of employment, present occupational status.
2) Educational achievement following discharge.
3) Marriages and divorces.

6. *Comparability:* Establishment of a reasonable presumption of comparability among delinquent groups is crucial. Such is the first and the most difficult part of the investigation. The task is difficult, in part at least, because we have no clear concept as to what constitutes comparability in these matters. This issue must be resolved in some acceptable manner, otherwise any interpretation of comparative statistics will be nonsense. Three approaches to the problems of comparability will be utilized in the study plans outlined below:

a. Matching groups upon characteristics which previous studies have indicated or suggested to be prognostically significant for delinquent youth.
b. Random sampling—where the concept appears appropriate.

7. *General Design:* The various plans outlined below have the same basic design:

a. Formation of comparison groups:
1) Select criteria for forming groups.
2) Screening case history material for data necessary to form comparison groups.

3) Analysis of screening data and formation of groups.

4) Selection of comparison criteria.

5) Collection of data for comparing effects of management.

6) Analysis of data.

b. Recommended criteria for comparing groups have been outlined in Section 5.

8. *Comparison between delinquents at Highfields during the early years of the project with delinquents at Annandale shortly before the Highfields Program began:*

a. Screening criteria:

1) Consider only delinquents at each facility during the first two or three years of the Highfields program. This will be necessary to permit reasonably long-term follow up at this time.

2) Follow same plan at Annandale but begin screening commitments during the month prior to the opening of Highfields and work back (in time) until an adequate sample has been secured.

3) Consider only cases at Annandale meeting designated criteria for admission to Highfields.

b. Selection of groups: Prognostic devices described below can be utilized.

1) On all cases passing screening criteria, collect specific data considered useful for predicting recidivism in delinquency.

2) Eliminate cases from both groups until the groups appear comparable according to given criteria.

c. Comments:

1) Presumably many of the boys at Highfields would have been sent to Annandale had the Highfields facilities been unavailable. Hence, it may be suspected that if we look at the Annandale population shortly before Highfields opened, more cases similar to the Highfields group could be found than would be the situation later.

2) If the assumption above is correct, there should be good prospects of finding a group at Annandale comparable to the Highfields group.

3) While it is true that delinquency rates vary in time, the possibility of error arising from the difference between time of commitment of the two groups appears to be a small matter compared with the selectivity which might be expected if the Annandale population is sampled after Highfields was implemented.

B. DATA ANALYSIS

1. *Data Obtained:*

a. Selection of cases. It was decided to restrict the selection of the cases for this study to boys who had the poorest prognoses. The boys who resided in and were sent to both facilities from Essex County were chosen.[26] Essex County is dominated by the city of Newark, which is a highly industrialized area. This county, which has the highest delinquency rate in the state, handles over one-third of all juvenile court cases in the state each year. Also, it supplies the bulk of the inmate population at all of the state correctional facilities as well.

The Annandale cases include boys who were committed from July, 1946 through June, 1950. The Highfields cases were boys who were admitted from July, 1950 through February, 1954.

A further selection of the cases was made by eliminating from the study boys who made poor adjustments in both facilities. At Highfields this group included boys who were returned to court for another disposition. At Annandale it included boys who fulfilled all of the criteria for admission

---

[26] Essex County is the seventh largest county government by population in the United States. In 1950 it had a population of over 900,000 people, 22 municipalities, and covered an area of 126 square miles. The juvenile court is administered by two judges who, in addition to domestic relations cases, handle more than 2,500 cases per year, of which 90 percent are boys between the ages of 8 and 17 years.

Sources: *Annual Report For 1955* of the Essex County Juvenile and Domestic Relations Court and *Children in New Jersey Juvenile Court—1954,* Bureau of Community Service of the N. J. Dept. of Institutions and Agencies, October 1955.

to Highfields but who received a rating of poor or very poor or who were transferred to the Reformatory for Older Males due to an unsatisfactory adjustment.

b. Number of cases: One Annandale Negro case was dropped from the study when it was found that he did not meet conditions specified for admission to Highfields. Hence this analysis was based upon the following number of cases: Annandale, 25 white and 24 Negro boys; Highfields, 25 white and 25 Negro boys.

c. Prognostic data: Data was obtained on all cases from official records.

d. Criteria data: Information from records was obtained on all cases for the following items:

1) Education following release
2) Marital status
3) Date of court action or parole suspension
4) Offense (court designation)
5) Court action for recidivists

In only four cases was other than routine classification into exposure or recidivism groups necessary.[27] We are reasonably sure that these data are fairly accurate insofar as history of delinquency following release, leading to court action or parole suspension, is concerned. Most recidivists were recommitted to New Jersey institutions for correction, although a few were committed to the Federal Reformatory at Chillicothe and one was committed to prison in another state. A few others were given warnings or fines or were placed on probation.

Data with respect to employment are less complete. Informa-

---

[27] One Highfields white was recorded as nonrecidivist; he voluntarily committed himself to a hospital for narcotics addiction. One Annandale white was recorded as nonrecidivist because there was no record of recidivism, although follow-up information that he entered the Marine Corps is not borne out by the Marine Corps, which has no record of his enlistment.

One Annandale Negro is listed as nonrecidivist; there is no record of recidivism, but he has been missing (and discharged from parole) since a year after his release. He has been recorded only in the one-year exposure group. One Highfields Negro has been recorded as exposed for less than two years and is in the less than eighteen months recidivism group because out of three years between release and recidivism he was committed to a hospital for 22 months.

tion on extent of unemployment and number of jobs held since release was least complete for cases with records of recidivism. Dates of employment could not be obtained; since employment data cannot be corrected for exposure time, it is, therefore, subject to only limited interpretation.

TABLE 8

Court Disposition Following First Recidivism
Annandale and Highfields

	White		Negro	
Disposition	Ann.	High.	Ann.	High.
Warning, fine, probation	4	2	2	3
Annandale	8	3	10	4
Bordentown	2	1	2	1
State prison	1	1	3 *	1
Action, military court			2	1
Federal Reformatory	1			1
City or county jail	2	1	2	

* One to North Carolina State Prison.

2. *Recidivism:*

Recidivism data were by far the most consistently obtained criteria data and appear the least difficult to interpret. Hence this report is largely concerned with comparative recidivism rates among delinquents released from the two institutions.

  a. Basis for tabulating recidivism rates. An individual has been considered a recidivist under either conditions below:

  1) He has been convicted for delinquency during the exposure period regardless of the court action.

  2) He is returned to the institution for parole violation. This situation can occur for Annandale cases only. Actually only one Negro and one—or possibly two [28]—whites were returned to Annandale for parole violation without court action; consequently for practical purposes this distinction between the situation of Annandale and Highfields cases is of little importance.

---

[28] Data on the second white case is not clear.

b. Overall recidivism rates. Recidivism rates for four exposure periods—twelve, twenty-four, thirty-six, and sixty months—appear in Table 9.[29] Recidivism among the Highfields group was consistently lower for both races and overall exposure periods. We note the rate is generally higher among Negroes than among whites.

TABLE 9

Exposures and Recidivists for Delinquents Released from Annandale and Highfields

Exposure Time	12 months Ann.	12 months High.	24 months Ann.	24 months High.	36 months Ann.	36 months High.	60 months Ann.	60 months High.
White								
Exposures	25	25	25	25	25	25	24	12
Recidivists	6	3	10	7	14	8	17	6
Negro								
Exposures	24	25	23	22	23	10	23	4
Recidivists	10	6	18	7	20	6	21	3
All Cases								
Exposures	49	50	48	47	48	35	47	16
Recidivists	16	9	28	14	34	14	38	9
Percent recidivists	33	18	58	30	71	40	79	56

To interpret the results as indicating that delinquents respond more favorably to treatment at Highfields requires two assumptions:

1) that recidivism rates constitute a valid index of post-treatment delinquency;
2) that groups from the two institutions are comparable recidivism risks apart from institutional effects.

c. Validity of criteria. If recidivism rates are to be taken as measures of delinquency following release from the two institutions, it must be assumed that public policy regarding detection of delinquency is comparable for the two groups.

---

[29] Unadjusted data on recidivism are in Table 10.

TABLE 10

Total Recidivism among Delinquents Released
from Annandale and Highfields
(Uncorrected for Exposure Time)

	White	Negro
Annandale		
No. cases	25	24
Recidivists	18	21
Highfields		
No. cases	25	25
Recidivists	9	11

A list of recidivism offenses and a list of court dispositions of
recidivists [30] does not suggest that the Annandale group usually committed less serious delinquencies. Beyond this data
we are without bases for evaluating the assumption above.[31]

d. Comparability among groups.

   1) Time between first offense and admission. It is generally
      assumed that the prognosis is less favorable for delin-
      quents with a long history of delinquent behavior prior
      to commitment than it is in cases where the history of
      delinquency is relatively brief.

Table 12 suggests that this relationship obtains in our data. For
instance, of 32 cases admitted within the first year, there were 8
cases of recidivism within two years of exposure, whereas of 23
admitted within the second year after a first offense there were
13 cases of recidivism within two years exposure. There is, however, no marked or consistent difference in proportion of recidivists (within 24 months) between the groups with 12 to 24, 24 to
48, and over 48 months between first offense and admission. It
seems reasonable, therefore, to control for time between first
offense and admission in terms of a dichotomy—(a) 0–12 months
and (b) over 12 months between first offense and admission.

---

[30] Refer to Table 8.
[31] We note in this connection that Annandale cases were released up to eight
years prior to the Highfields cases. Boys released from Annandale were under
the supervision of parole officers, whereas Highfields cases reported to probation officers.

TABLE 11

Offenses (First Recidivism) of Delinquents Released
from Annandale and Highfields

	White		Negro	
	Ann.	High.	Ann.	High.
A. *Offenses against Persons*				
Assault and battery	3		2	
Assault, attempted robbery		1		1
Carnal abuse	1		2	
Concealed weapons	1			1
Immorality				1
Rape	1			
Robbery			1	1
B. *Offenses against Property*				
B & E			4	1
BE & L	2			
BEL & R		3		
Burglary			1	
Larceny	1	2	4	
Auto larceny	1			
Mail theft				1
Receiving stolen goods	1			
C. *Offenses against Public Policy*				
Disorderly conduct	2	1	3	1
Driving without license	1	1		
Motor Vehicle Law	2		1	1
Nonsupport	1			
Narcotics			1	2
D. *Other Offenses*				
AWOL			2	1
Murder	1			
Multiple recidivists	5	2	6	3

TABLE 12

Exposures and Recidivists for 24-Months Exposure Time By Time between First Court Record and Admission

Time between First Record and Admission.

	0–12 mo.		Over 12 to 24 mo.		Over 24 to 48 mo.		Over 48 mo.	
	Ann.	High.	Ann.	High.	Ann.	High.	Ann.	High.
White								
Exposures	2	14	7	4	8	4	8	3
Recidivists	0	3	4	1	2	2	4	1
Negro								
Exposures	5	11	6	6	8	1	4	4
Recidivists	2	3	5	3	7	0	4	1
Both Races								
Exposures	7	25	13	10	16	5	12	7
Recidivists	2	6	9	4	9	2	8	2

The results appear in Tables 15 and 16. Only 7 Annandale cases had 12 months or less between the time of first recorded offense and admission; hence intergroup comparisons for boys with shorter histories of delinquency are of limited value for statistical purposes.

TABLE 13

Exposures and Recidivists for 12-months Exposure Time By Time between First Court Record and Admission

Time between First Offense and Admission

	0–12 mo.		Over 12 to 24 mo.		Over 24 to 48 mo.		Over 48 mo.	
	Ann.	High.	Ann.	High.	Ann.	High.	Ann.	High.
White								
Exposures	2	14	7	4	8	4	8	3
Recidivists	—	2	2	—	2	—	2	1
Negro								
Exposures	5	12	6	8	8	1	5	4
Recidivists	—	3	2	2	4	—	4	4

TABLE 14

Exposures and Recidivists for 36-Months Exposure Time
By Time between First Court Record and Admission

Time between First Offense and Admission

	0–12 mo. Ann.	0–12 mo. High.	Over 12 to 24 mo. Ann.	Over 12 to 24 mo. High.	Over 24 to 48 mo. Ann.	Over 24 to 48 mo. High.	Over 48 mo. Ann.	Over 48 mo. High.
White								
Exposures	2	14	7	4	8	4	8	3
Recidivists	1	4	4	1	3	2	6	1
Negro								
Exposures	5	5	5	2	9	—	4	3
Recidivists	3	3	5	1	8	—	4	2

Considering delinquents with more than one year between first delinquency and admission, the Highfields group consistently shows a lower proportion of recidivists. This holds for both Negro and white delinquents at 12, 24, and 36 months exposure.

TABLE 15

Exposures and Recidivists for Delinquents Released
from Annandale and Highfields: One Year or Less
between First Offense and Admission

Exposure Time	12 months Ann.	12 months High.	24 months Ann.	24 months High.	36 months Ann.	36 months High.	60 months Ann.	60 months High.
White								
Exposures	2	14	2	14	2	14	2	6
Recidivists	0	2	0	3	1	4	2	2
Negro								
Exposures	5	12	5	11	5	5		
Recidivists	0	3	2	3	3	3		
Both Races								
Exposures	7	26	7	26	7	19		
Recidivists	0	5	2	5	4	7		

TABLE 16

Exposures and Recidivists for Delinquents Released
from Annandale and Highfields: More than One Year
between First Offense and Admission

Exposure Time	12 months		24 months		36 months		60 months	
	Ann.	High.	Ann.	High.	Ann.	High.	Ann.	High.
White								
Exposures	23	11	23	11	23	11	22	6
Recidivists	6	1	10	4	13	4	15	4
Negro								
Exposures	19	13	18	11	18	5		
Recidivists	10	3	16	4	17	3		
Both Races								
Exposures	42	24	41	22	41	16		
Recidivists	16	4	26	8	30	7		

The differences are statistically significant at the .05 level for
the following comparison groups: Negro (24-months exposure)
and both races combined (12 and 36-months exposure).[32] In other
(comparisons samples were too small to establish significant differences, although the difference in recidivism rates for the two
institutions was quite striking in some cases. At a 60-month exposure period recidivism rates among the white delinquents
released from the two institutions appear quite similar; the number of Highfields cases with 60 months exposure is too small to
warrant inference.[33]

---

[32] Chi-square test with one degree of freedom.
Significance tests have not been applied to the sub-sample of delinquents
admitted within the first year of their first offense because the samples from
Annandale were generally too small to permit a valid Chi-square. It is possible but unlikely that some information could be extracted from those data
with exact significance tests. It is of interest to note that, within the fragments
of information available about cases admitted within 12 months of their first
offense, the consistent trend in favor of the Highfields groups seen above does
not obtain. Most pronounced, of 5 Annandale Negroes there were no recidivists
within 12 months, whereas of 12 Highfields Negroes there were 3 recidivists
within the first 12 months.
[33] So few Highfields Negroes had 5 years exposure that we have omitted comparison.

2) Education. Table 17 does not imply that the differences between the recidivism rates for the Annandale and Highfields groups are due to differences in the educational levels of the two groups.

3) Marital status, residence, and age at admission. Similarly, Table 18 suggests that the differences are not accounted for in terms of advantages of the Highfields group in marital status of parents, residence, or age at admission.

e. Conclusion: Recidivism rates among Highfields versus Annandale groups: Recidivism rates among delinquents re-

TABLE 17

Exposures and Recidivists for Delinquents with Record
of Offense More than 12 Months Prior to Admission
By Race, Exposure Time, and Educational Level

Exposure Time	12 months Ann.	12 months High.	24 months Ann.	24 months High.	36 months Ann.	36 months High.
Eighth Grade or Below						
White						
Exposures	14	8	14	8	14	8
Recidivists	4	1	7	3	8	3
Negro						
Exposures	9	10	9	8	9	4
Recidivists	6	3	9	4	9	3
Both races						
Exposures	23	18	23	16	23	12
Recidivists	10	4	16	7	17	6
Ninth Grade or Above						
White						
Exposures	9	3	9	3	9	3
Recidivists	2	1	3	1	5	1
Negro						
Exposures	10	3	9	3	8	1
Recidivists	4	0	7	0	7	0
Both races						
Exposures	19	6	18	6	17	4
Recidivists	6	0	10	1	12	1

TABLE 18

Exposures and Recidivists for 24-Months Exposure Period (all cases) by Race, Marital Status of Parents, Residence, and Age at Admission

	White Ann.	High.	Negro Ann.	High.	Both Races Ann.	High.
Marital Status of Parents						
Home broken						
Exposures	11	9	20	9	31	18
Recidivists	5	1	16	4	21	5
Home not broken						
Exposures	14	16	3	13	17	29
Recidivists	5	6	2	3	7	9
Residence at Admission						
Newark						
Exposures	20	16	19	18	39	34
Recidivists	5	6	15	7	20	13
Not Newark						
Exposures	5	8	4	4	9	12
Recidivists	5	1	3	0	8	4
Age at Admission						
16 yrs. or less						
Exposures	0	5	0	3	0	8
Recidivists	0	3	0	2	0	5
Over 16 to 17						
Exposures	16	12	15	15	31	27
Recidivists	7	3	12	3	19	6
Over 17 to 18						
Exposures	9	8	8	4	17	12
Recidivists	3	1	6	2	9	3

leased from Highfields were substantially lower than rates among the Annandale group. This obtains for four exposure periods: 12, 24, 36, and 60 months.[34] Part of the difference may be explained in terms of the fact that Highfields often

---

[34] Three month and six-month exposure periods were considered, but in neither case were there enough recidivists to warrant conclusions.

appeared to receive cases which were favorable risks when compared to delinquents admitted to Annandale, the most pronounced differences being that Highfields received a larger number of cases with a short time between first recorded delinquency (court appearance) and admission to the institution. However, when the samples are stratified to adjust for difference between first offense and admission as well as several other variables commonly considered prognostic—age at admission, education, residence, and marital status of parents—the Highfields group still has substantially fewer recidivists, at least for the first three years of exposure.[35]

f. Further observations.

1) Race: Recidivism was more frequent among Negroes than among white boys. This held for delinquents released from both Annandale and Highfields.

2) Residence: For white boys, the contrast in recidivism rates between Annandale and Highfields could be attributed entirely to delinquents whose homes were outside the city of Newark (Table 18). This relation did not obtain for Negroes.

3) Prognosis and Highfields advantage: Certain items of data suggest that the delinquents most likely to benefit from Highfields are those who would have the poorest prognosis when released from Annandale—or those who are regarded generally as poor risks.

(a) Highfields rates were more favorable with delinquents having a long history of delinquency.

(b) Highfields rates were more favorable with delinquents from broken homes (white group).

(c) Highfields rates were more favorable with older delinquents (white group).

---

[35] In addition to the control indicated above we have considered:
(1) Whether or not a delinquent returned home after release (upon the assumption that delinquents who had homes to receive them might be less likely to recidivize). All but one or two cases in our sample returned home.
(2) Type of offense for which delinquents were committed.

XI

Problems in Administration

IT HAS BEEN ALMOST AS DIFFICULT TO RELATE THE STORY OF HIGH-fields in this report as it was for the boy who attempted to impart to his girl friend, in a telephone conversation, the meaning of his experiences in the guided group interaction sessions. He said, "Hon, last night the meeting skinned me. They really chewed me out, they poured it on so thick and fast, I almost forgot who I was." She asked, "But why do they have to be so mean to you?" He replied, "See I've tried and tried to tell you what Highfields is all about but you don't understand. They have to be mean to me. I want them to be mean to me or I'll never get any help. When you come up on Sunday, I'll try to explain it all over again." However, difficult as it has been, we have found in our work with the boys, the courts and their probation officers, the public and other state agencies, that the fears and the skepticism many persons may have felt about the program never really materialized. Instead, we have discovered time and again that the hopes and hard work of a small group of people created a thoroughly satisfactory and fruitful program. As each therapy group prepares to return to the community, it is possible to look back and recall, as the group itself does, the initial fumbling and aimlessness, the later struggles and discouragement, and the final excitement in discovering that problems can be resolved, attitudes changed, and new self-concepts created. The fact that adolescent offenders are able to achieve these results in the relatively short period of four months may raise many issues in the field of correction and possibly in other areas. In fact, it would be interesting to speculate on the implications of the program. However, it is neither our function nor our intent to do so here. Rather, we have tried to record our experiences at Highfields as we have lived them from the inception of the program, through a period of a few short years. Of course, when one considers that most of the correctional facilities in the United States were built over a hundred years ago, five years is too brief a span of time to view and evaluate the role of Highfields in American penology. In this chapter, we propose to consider some of the major problems we have encountered in the day-to-day operation of the program. Public agencies, legislators, administrators, and professional workers in the field of correction who may be in a position to consider the possibility of embarking upon this kind of a program may be interested in the practical administrative problems of Highfields.

It is safe to assume that no treatment facility dealing with youthful offenders today is operating in an ideal setting. For, not only is it extremely difficult to foresee all of the major issues that will arise in the future course of operations, it is also presumptuous to assume that the present state of knowledge about the causes and treatment of youthful offenders is so advanced that we can afford to declare a moritorium on research activities, and claim that "now we can truly establish the perfect program for the reformation of our antisocial youths." It is important to permit experimentation with currently established concepts. In fact, the practical realities of everyday living require that some of these ideas be applied. However, at the same time, we must be careful to avoid the encrustation of our programs and our ideas merely because we are fearful of future consequences. Perhaps in few other fields of human endeavor has man been so cautious of change as he has been in the field of correction. It would be short-sighted indeed to regard these practical problems as being mutually exclusive. Few of them at Highfields are so separate and distinct from each other, even though each of them may seem to be of an entirely separate character, that they can be treated apart from one another. When a boy gets upset in a group session and afterwards deliberately throws a rock through one of the windows, can we deal with each incident separately? Some of these problems involve the formal structure of the program, while others revolve around the informal relationships between the people who live in and work at Highfields. Actually, there is a merging of formalities with the less formal and even purely informal aspects of the program. However, for purposes of analysis, it is possible to categorize the problems in terms of their origins. Some of them can be viewed as having their sources outside of the facility and are regarded as extramural problems; others originate within Highfields itself and are defined as intramural problems.

Of the three types of extramural problems we have encountered, perhaps the most crucial one in terms of its potential damage has been the pressure to "institutionalize" the program. Whenever a new agency or department is incorporated into a larger administrative structure, efforts are directed to insure that it will adhere to the established practices of the parent unit, that it play a role that is consistent with the policies and procedures of all of the other subsidiary units. We have had a similar experience at Highfields. In 1952, when the project formally became a part of the New Jersey state correctional system, pressures external to Highfields were exerted to reorganize its administrative structure to conform to that of each of the other correctional institutions. Acceptance of this plan would have meant the establishment of a Board of Managers to set policies for and oversee the operation of the program. A Board of Managers is a policy-making body at each institution consisting of unpaid citizens appointed by the Governor for a fixed term of office. The superintendent of each institution is appointed by this board and serves at their pleasure as their representative. In all institutions except the State Prison this unit is also a paroling authority. As it is now constituted, the administration of Highfields is supervised directly by the Director of Correction and Parole of the State Department of Institutions and Agencies. This attempt to bureaucratize the relationship between the project and the department would have set the pattern for the institutionalization of Highfields. It would have meant that all important decisions about each boy as well as about the various segments of the program would have had to be submitted to this group for their approval. However, the program operates in such a way that crucial decisions regarding these and other matters must be made almost daily. For example, when a boy is returned to court for another disposition he must leave immediately regardless of the time of day. To prolong his departure by waiting for a Board of Managers' decision would create problems of supervision for the staff which they would not be able to resolve. For the other boys it might mean, as it has, a continued threat to them which would impede the progress of their careers.

Moreover, there are indirect pressures from the central office of the department to cast the administration into a bureaucratic mold. Almost daily, the department issues memoranda, administrative orders, reports, forms, and records which are designed to standardize the practices and enhance the operating efficiency of the institutions. While not all of these orders apply to Highfields, oftentimes it is necessary to file reports and keep records of data that are of little importance to the facility. From 1950 until 1952 when the State assumed direct responsibility for the program, apart from daily correspondence, the director was required to prepare two sets of reports, a monthly statement on the earnings of each boy, and a monthly report to the courts and probation departments on each boy's adjustment. Three years later, these reports had increased to ten, along with additional records of a bookkeeping nature.

Indirect pressures to formalize the program have taken other forms as well. Periodically, since 1952, state inspectors have appeared to investigate various matters, such as the type and quantities of food served, the size and depth of the garbage pits, the shower curtains and the storeroom, posting of rules and regulations on the walls and placing of signs on the doors, the landscaping, the laundry situation, housekeeping, and haircuts for the boys as well as uniforms and sewage disposal. These functionaries have been carrying out their responsibilities each time they have made demands on the program to conform to departmental standards. It has been the responsibility of the directors of Highfields to maintain a proper balance between the standards of cleanliness and health of the boys and staff and the maintenance of the program. In effect, this responsibility involves a problem of continually interpreting the program to each visitor, official and unofficial. However, it has been the departmental official directly responsible for Highfields who has successfully performed this task at the higher levels of government. Over the years, the Director of Correction and Parole has fended off the extramural pressures by interpreting the relationship of the program to the state correctional system. He has had to explain it continuously to new executive officials, legislators, and other public officials as well as to professional bodies and private associations.

From time to time, suggestions have been made to modify the schedule of activities by introducing some of the features that are usually found in a modern correctional institution, such as self-government, casework and psychological services, an orientation program, and others. We are not prepared to state whether or not some of these services would enhance the effectiveness of our work. Only further experience and research will confirm or deny it. However, within the limitations of our present knowledge about youthful offenders and the objectives of the program, we have avoided the introduction of these features. For example, a boy who comes to Highfields will find that no attempt is made to rigidly structure his daily activities or his interpersonal activities. From the very moment of his admission, until the day he leaves, he learns that Highfields is not an imposing, complex, bureaucratized facility. The gap between his life in the community and his experiences at Highfields is bridged by himself, in his own way, for no formal effort is made to introduce him to the program by subjecting him to a period of formal orientation and fact finding. He is neither intensely interviewed nor tested by any member of the staff. There is no period of quarantine, no uniform, no school, no vocational training, no organized recreation, no rule book, no signs, notices, posters, or labels. Through experience and contact with other boys and employees, each new admission develops a conception of Highfields which becomes an integral part of the way in which he interacts with the people and the program. The absence of a schedule of activities that accounts for every moment of the day is an integral feature of the Highfields design.

Instead of concerning himself with the complex features of the program and developing ways and means of coping with them, the boy at Highfields has an opportunity to concern himself with his own problems and to select those features which he can utilize to help him cope with his problems. In order to work toward this objective, the daily schedule must be organized so as to permit the boys in residence to select their own associates and create their own activities. When one boy stated, as most of them do, that, "There's nothing to do around here, no T.V., no swimming, no nothing. It's so boring, I get sick of this place," an older group member pointed out, "There's plenty to do around here. Believe me. There isn't enough time to work on all your problems. If all you want to do is play games, and have people tell you what to do and when to do it, then you don't belong here." This is a problem for each boy to deal with. In some respects the way in which he meets it, is an indication of the kind of adjustment he is making.

Of course, some members of the staff and boys, too, occasionally attempt to introduce measures of a formal, institutionalized nature, particularly in the area of rewards and punishments. As indicated in a previous chapter, the cottage parents succeeded in structuring their relationships with the boys by introducing a system of punishment called "hours in the pit." Also, as a last resort in dealing with a difficult boy they will threaten to "send you to the office." The work supervisor, too, has devised his own system of control, which includes "putting boys on report." This means that he puts a boy's name on a slip of paper or merely that he will make special mention of the boy to the director. When a new employee arrives, sooner or later, some of the boys will ask "Why don't you give us hours in the pit?" At other times, boys have demanded that a system of conventional reward and punishment be established, ". . . to make it easier for us to understand what we can do and can't do. The way things are now, you don't know when you're doing something wrong." One boy insisted on talking to the director about this situation as it applied to him. He stated, "Why don't you talk to me about the things I'm doing around here, the way you talk to some of the other boys. I know

I get into trouble, but nobody says anything about it. I'd feel better if you told me about the things I'm doing because I'm getting worried." Also, it is characteristic of boys who have had institutional experience to insist that, "It would be better if you put down a list of all the rules the way they do at X——. That way you'd get your punishment when you broke the rules and it would be all over. This way you always think about what you did." The fact that there is no formal system to regulate the behavior of the boys results in additional work for the employees, in the sense that they are continually being forced to interpret the meaning of each act in terms of the objectives of the program rather than in terms of a predetermined set of rules and regulations.

We have tried to create a social world which enables the boys to reorganize their conceptions of themselves, restructure their group affiliations, and test a wide range of attitudes, social roles, personalities, and group situations. In order to preserve the informal and nonthreatening character of life at the project, it has been necessary to sensitize ourselves to various efforts which would bureaucratize it—whether such efforts involve increased specialization of the roles of each employee or increased professional staff, rigidifying the hierarchy of authority by circumscribing it so strictly that individual employees find it very difficult and even uncomfortable to make decisions, establishing a system of abstract rules to insure uniformity of performance by each boy, or conducting the program in "a spirit of formalistic impersonality, . . . without hatred or passion and hence without affection or enthusiasm" [36] by developing a detached, aloof attitude toward the problems of the boys. This position does not mean that the program as it is now constituted is inviolate. Modification in the design of the program can and should be made in the light of experience and research findings. A large and increasing number of areas of our lives are being spent within the framework of the complex mechanisms of highly structured organizations. Without

[36] Max Weber, *The Theory of Social and Economic Organization*, translated by A. M. Henderson and Talcott Parsons. New York: Oxford University Press, 1947, p. 331.

much effort, Highfields could be transformed into a small bureaucratic unit such as is found in many forestry camps and small treatment centers for youthful offenders. It may be necessary for these units to maintain a purely bureaucratic type of administrative organization in the interests of efficiency; however, our experience has been that increased rationalization of the program frustrates our efforts. Moreover, since our paramount consideration is the welfare of the boys in residence, we must be aware of the effect of the structure of the correctional community on the individual boy as well as the role of this community as an active force in treatment.

Still another problem of an extramural nature involves the relationship between Highfields and other official agencies. The fact that boys are not committed, but rather live at Highfields as a condition of their probation, means that a close liaison must be maintained with the county juvenile courts and probation departments. The selection of boys for admission rests with the juvenile court judges, and it is very important that the boys who are best suited for residence are chosen. The program is flexible enough to carry a few boys, such as a feeble-minded or a previously institutionalized boy, who do not fulfill all of the criteria for admission, but whether or not these boys are able to survive at Highfields depends, in large measure, on the social climate of the home. Some groups are able to absorb these boys into their activities and therapy groups in a way that is of benefit to all, other groups are not so able. The fact that these judges have accepted the idea that some boys will turn out to be unsuitable for residence and therefore returned to court for another disposition, permits the admission of such cases. Our experience indicates that the injudicious selection of cases for admission can be detrimental to the program and in turn to the boys themselves. However, evidence that it is possible to acquaint judges with the program and to secure their utmost cooperation can be found in our dealings with the juvenile court judges in New Jersey. They have been sympathetic, helpful, and enthusiastic about Highfields. In many respects they have set the pace in encouraging other persons, especially the parents of the boys, to accept Highfields as a positive

approach in correction. Probation officers, too, have played a leading role in this regard. Not only is it necessary to work closely
with each boy's probation officer through correspondence, visits,
telephone, and monthly reports, but, frequently, probation officers, like the judges, sit in on the guided group interaction sessions to gain firsthand information on the operation of the program. The following statement by a probation officer who supported Highfields very strongly from the outset sums up the
attitude of many of the probation officers who have supervised
Highfields boys.

Bergen County has taken an active interest in the Highfields Treatment Center since its inception.

We immediately recognized it as a source of treatment, which, if
capably handled by a probation officer, would have lasting effect. Accordingly, almost immediately, we developed what we considered sound
practices and policies within our own organization in connection with
the boys sent to Highfields and those awaiting transfer or awaiting available space for them at Highfields.

We decided on preparing a boy for this experience. We told him of
the "break" for him and the great opportunities he would have in his
approximately four months residence at Highfields; of the opportunity
to get good work habits, the opportunity to "talk through" his personal and family problems, of the benefit that would accrue to him
physically.

We told him that we expected him to enter into all of the activities
at the project including the "bull sessions." We told him something of
the Institute and the history connected with the old Lindbergh home.
We informed him of the pay that he would receive and what he could
purchase with it. He was informed about the possibility of furlough
and of visitors. He knew pretty much what to expect from those who
would be there in an official capacity and from the other boys there,
who needed help, like he.

And above all, he was told that his probation officer would take
him to Highfields, see him frequently, and not forget him.

This preparation helped both the boy and the probation officer in
their personal relationships.

It also helped the parents, in advance of the boy's going, to know
that he was going to a selected project, with no bars or guards and
where there were many advantages over a penal institution.

So, with this preparation, a team was formed to work with this boy, which circulated from the judge of the juvenile court to the probation officer to the director of Highfields and then back to the judge, et cetera.

The probation officer made frequent visits to the boys at Highfields, sometimes unannounced. He kept his part of the bargain. From these interviews and from observing the boys at work came matters to be discussed with the parents. We were able to prepare the parents for their son's furlough and eventual return to the home. Sometimes, we were able to correct a home situation before the lad returned.

Reports from the director to the judge and probation officer were used as an instrument for good; to encourage the boys who were having difficulty accepting the project and to point up the needs of others. We were able to discover certain weaknesses, anxieties and hostilities which needed attention; his ability or lack of it to get along with his peers. Some boys were able to make plans while at Highfields for a continuation of their studies in high school and the probation officer arranged for this.[37]

The design of the program is such that support is necessary and must be forthcoming from the central office of the State Department of Institutions and Agencies as well as from other state institutions. The Commissioner and the Director of Correction and Parole provide assistance by interpreting the program to the State Board of Control, the state agency that estalishes general policies and procedures for all the state institutions, to the executive and legislative branches of the state government, to the press and the public. Other institutions provide services that Highfields cannot offer. For example, the State Neuro-Psychiatric Institute provides a work situation and emergency medical care for the boys as well as bookkeeping and other business office assistance, the State Prison at Trenton offers weekly laundry service, and the Trenton State Hospital assists in immunizing every admission. The close support which these officials and institutions give Highfields is invaluable.

Still another and equally crucial problem is the role of community relations. The attitude of the citizens of the borough of

[37] Statement of Mr. Walter A. Penfield, *Eighth Public Hearings* of the New Jersey State Juvenile Delinquency Study Commission, February 3, 1956, pp. 60A–61A.

Hopewell, the nearest community to the project, is as important to the success of Highfields as is any part of the program. They provide an opportunity for contact with the normal life of conventional citizens. Ordinarily, very few inmates of correctional institutions are able to take advantage of the goods and services of the outside world. In Hopewell, the local newspaper, the *Borough Council,* the Chief of Police, the tradesmen, the local physician who examines the boys, the Garden Club, the Women's Club, and the neighbors have been very sympathetic in providing services which Highfields cannot possibly offer, and very helpful in times of trouble. As a result, the boys are able to make purchases, phone calls, attend church, have their hair cut, their clothes cleaned, visit the theater, and satisfy other personal requirements.

All of these extramural problems—the pressures to institutionalize the program, the need for close support of judges, probation officers, state officials, and institutions, and the important of community relationships—must be considered in the administration of Highfields. The very fact of their existence highlights the kind of balance that must be achieved to operate and define not only the program but the role that people outside of Highfields play in the lives of every boy.

Another set of problems originates within Highfields itself. There are four major types of these intramural problems— namely, personnel, finance, maintenance, and special problems that involve the boys in residence.

We have indicated in several instances the key role that the staff, in a very direct sense, plays in the treatment process. The fact that there are only six employees to supervise twenty boys makes it possible for each boy to develop a fairly close relationship with them. The presence of innumerable adults in a correctional facility makes it virtually impossible for the inmates to develop intimate, meaningful ties with staff members. On occasion an inmate may become friendly with one or two staff members he feels are "helping" him. However, he realizes that the important decisions in his case will be executed by persons with whom he cannot possibly develop a close bond. The warden, the parole board, the classification committee members—these are staff members who by the very nature of their roles and functions cannot relate with inmates except in a formal, impersonal sense. Moreover, membership in the inmate social system precludes the establishment of the kind of relationships between staff and inmate that can be therapeutic.[38]

At Highfields, the roles and functions of all of the staff members, except the secretary, are neither rigidly formalized by the administrative structure nor circumscribed by a set of abstract rules and regulations. An employee is able to relate with each boy in his own way, within the circle of his own abilities and limitations. There is an overlapping of roles by the staff members. For example, in addition to acting as an authority figure, as all employees do, the cook prepares meals and advises boys; her husband, the cottage supervisor, acts as handyman, a friend, and a supervisor; the director conducts the group sessions, cooks, supervises boys directly and administers the program; the work supervisor assigns jobs and takes the boy to the movies; the intern may play all of these roles at one time or another. Also, the boys' social system is so diffuse, partly because of the fairly rapid turnover and partly because of the kinds of roles which "old boys" play in it, that actually it serves to encourage communication and close relationships with staff members. Of course, it is important for the staff members to maintain a social distance between themselves and the boys which is consistent with their roles as adults who have a job to perform and as authority figures who are working with boys in trouble. The fact that the director, the intern, and the cottage parents reside in the same building and eat the same meals with the boys helps to reinforce the close ties that develop between most of the boys and the staff.

The problem of financing the program is of real concern to everyone—legislators, judges, state officials, and taxpayers alike. In many instances the cost of maintaining correctional facilities is regarded as so excessive as to be unwarranted. In order to evaluate the program at Highfields on this level, we will present in

---

[38] For a discussion of this problem in a custodial institution see L. W. McCorkle and R. Korn, "Resocialization Within Walls," *Annals*, May 1954, pp. 88–91.

the following section a consideration of the financial operations of Highfields.

As indicated in the first chapter, the program was undertaken initially as a cooperative venture of the New York Fund and the New Jersey Department of Institutions and Agencies. For a two year period starting in the summer of 1950, the former organization made a grant of $25,000 to Highfields to cover the cost of salaries and the State provided the facilities for conducting the program. Then, in July, 1952, the State of New Jersey assumed sole responsibility for Highfields and set up its first annual budget for the fiscal year, 1952–53.

A picture of the financial operation of the project for the three fiscal years covered in this report is presented in Table 19. An examination of the annual budget reveals that there has been a general increase in overall expenditures. From 1952 through the 1955 fiscal year, there was an increase of $3,655 in the total cost of maintaining the program. The major portion of this increase was in the salaries account, which rose from 52 percent of the total budget to 68.5 percent. This was due largely to the fact that an additional employee, a senior clerk-stenographer, was added to the staff in 1955. This action, in addition to the annual salary increments which every employee received, accounts for the substantial rise in expenditures for 1955 as compared with the previous fiscal year. Increased costs were experienced in another major account, namely, current repairs, which rose from 3.7 percent to 4.3 percent of the budget. However, the "Services Other Than Personal" category was the same in the first and in the last year, and the "Materials and Supplies" category decreased over 13 percent from 42 percent to 25.4 percent of all expenditures. This decrease was not surprising in view of the fact that a large portion of the funds in this account in 1952 was allotted for the purchase of furniture and other household supplies which do not have to be replaced annually.

The annual budget covers the cost of various items. In 1954–55, the last fiscal year covered in this report, the funds were distributed as follows: salaries and wages for six staff members, 68.5 percent; materials and supplies such as food, clothing, utilities, maintenance of the grounds, household items, transportation, laundry service, and stationery and office supplies, 25.4 percent; other services, including postage, insurance, telephone and telegraph, and travel expenses, 2.3 percent; and current repairs on the building as well as on a passenger car and a truck, 4.8 percent.

TABLE 19

Cost of Operation
By Categories and Fiscal Year

Fiscal Year	Total Cost in Dollars	Percent Salaries	Percent Materials and Supplies	Expenditures Percent Services Other Than Personal	Percent Current Repairs
1952–53	28,318	52.0	42.0	2.3	3.7
1953–54	29,839	58.9	35.4	2.0	3.7
1954–55	31,973	68.5	25.4	2.3	4.8

In interpreting these expenditures, it should be borne in mind that the business office of a nearby state hospital, the Neuro-Psychiatric Institute, maintains the bookkeeping records, makes purchases, and conducts other financial operations for Highfields. Moreover, the wages that the boys receive each week are supplied by the Institute, since they work for that institution and not for Highfields. In addition, as indicated earlier, the Institute provides emergency medical care for the boys in residence as well as for the employees. The fact that services are granted by other state institutions is an important consideration. It could be extremely burdensome to Highfields to pay for the services of both a business office and a medical staff and a laundry.

Of course, it is difficult to evaluate the financial cost of maintaining any public institution. Oftentimes, institutions will supplement their appropriations with farm and/or industrial production, gifts from individuals, and grants and donations from philanthropic foundations. In many respects then, the cost information of correctional facilities is elusive, inaccessible, and even subject to wide interpretations; in fact, it would be extremely difficult to compare the per capita costs of two or more correctional systems, since they rarely use comparable methods of cost accounting.[39] However, it should be noted that the design of the program, along with the assistance of other state facilities, makes it possible to keep the cost of maintaining a boy in residence at a minimum. Since the period of residence is about four months, the cost of supporting a single boy for this period has averaged $516 during the three-year period covered in the table above.

Some of the intramural problems are not easily apparent to a casual observer, for they are part and parcel of the daily life of the residents. They include the problem of the optimum size of the population, the role of the intern, social control, crises, runaways, and peer-group relationships. Although many of these problems are found in any correctional facility, others are peculiar to the Highfields situation.

It is characteristic of correctional institutions today that they are overcrowded. The increased size of the juvenile age group in this country has not been accompanied by a corresponding increase in correctional facilities. Overcrowding creates a myriad of problems, sometimes to the point where the program breaks down and the administration concerns itself primarily with custody. Highfields is no exception, for an increase in the population from eighteen to twenty-two boys usually results in a marked decrease in the effectiveness of the program. From the point of view of the individual boy, there are too many other boys to compete with. The meetings are so large that some boys feel lost and rejected. Too, it seems to take a longer period of time for the therapy groups to function properly. We have observed that a rise in the population beyond twenty boys is accompanied by an increase in the number and seriousness of hostile, aggressive acts. Not only do the boys become more anxious and defensive, but the employees become less patient, less willing to relate closely with the

---

[39] See Dr. Myrl E. Alexander, "Do Our Prisons Cost Too Much," *Annals* V 293, May 1954, pp. 35–41; and U. S. Children's Bureau, Statistical Series No. 33, *Some Facts About Public Training Schools for Juvenile Delinquents*, U. S. Government Printing Office: Wash., D. C., 1956, pp. 31–33, for a discussion of this problem.

boys, and more anxious of their ability to supervise them. This situation becomes apparent not only in the guided group interaction sessions but at work and in the peer-group activities around the house. Although it has been difficult to keep the population at a manageable level because of the pressure from the courts, our experience has shown that the optimum size is about eighteen boys.

It seems to be important also to maintain the program as an independent unit. The tendency to make large institutions even larger by adding more cottages or more wings is strong in the field of correction, particularly in the United States. To redesign the administrative structure by the addition of another building and thereby accommodate more boys would require modifications in the design of the program to such a degree that it would impair it seriously if not result, in effect, in the establishment of another conventional type of bureaucratic facility. The fact that boys are able to conceive of Highfields as a place that they can cope with is an indication of the necessity to keep intact the basic design of the program.[40]

Social control in a correctional facility is a problem of paramount important. Ordinarily, the administration relies on the walls or fences, printed rules and regulations, a custodial force, a disciplinary committee, segregation, self-government, guidance units, and other means to maintain order within the confines of the facility. At Highfields, control is achieved through a variety of techniques, but primarily through the conceptions that the boys and the staff have of each other. If boys perceive the adults as authorities who are oriented toward them in terms of rehabili-

---

[40] In an attempt to determine the impact of staff design on inmates in European correctional institutions, Reckless found that, "one . . . receives the distinct impression that while smallness of size (inmate population) is not a prerequisite for institutions designed to have constructive effect on inmate persons, yet smallness is certainly a great aid to effective operation of a program and simple design of staff which can reach the inmate. Small institutions can be simply staffed and simply operated. There are too many small institutions in Europe, which are considered by governmental departments as practical for the purposes at hand, to pass over the item of smallness in an off hand manner." Walter C. Reckless, "Lesson to Be Learned from Institutions for Delinquent Youth in Europe," *British Journal of Delinquency*, Vol. 7, No. 1, July 1956, pp. 66–77.

tation rather than punishment or deterrence or revenge, then they will be able, in time, to respond to the situation in similar terms. Of course, not all boys are able to conduct themselves in terms of the staff definition of the situation. However, by testing the situation and by internalizing the norms of Highfields, most boys learn to view it as the staff does. For example, one boy complained in a group meeting that one of the employees was picking on him. Another member of the group said to him, "When Pop tells you to do a job over or gives you hours, he's not picking on you. He's helping you. Can't you see that? It's no skin off his back because you don't clean the walls good. He's trying to teach you to do a job and you're fighting him. When you get out you won't be able to keep a job because the boss will fire you in a minute. There's no second chance. Pop is just helping you to do it right the first time."

This definition of the situation is reinforced by the guided group interaction sessions in which every boy has an opportunity to participate. The incentive to help oneself sufficiently to secure a release means that a premium is placed on the attitude "to tell the meeting everything about yourself." Moreover, boys feel that no consequence will follow from a defection from the rules if they relate it to the group. One boy described it in the following manner, "If you tell the group about the things you do, right or wrong, then the meeting knows that you want to help yourself. But if you hide things and we find out later, you'll never get out." The fact that boys can communicate with each other freely and frankly, without fear of reprisals, in the presence of the director has a stabilizing effect on the group members which carries over into the interpersonal relationships outside the meetings. As each therapy group moves forward in the direction of increased solidarity, the impact of the sessions becomes so great and, at times, so intense that the behavior of each member becomes a matter of concern for the entire group. When the members become oriented toward prosocial attitudes and values, their behavior, in turn, takes on a corresponding conventional character. Some group members take it upon themselves to "check" the conduct of fellow members, even to the point when a boy will complain, as many of them do that, "You guys are checking me too much. Everytime I do something somebody says 'I got you checked for this, I got you checked for that,' that's crazy." Also, "old boys" tend to scoff at the pranks and the hostile aggressive acts of "new boys," thereby exercising a measure of control over them. Of course, an indirect though very effective means of control is utilized by "old boys" who have changed. Not only do they set examples for other boys, but in a sense they are living proof that Highfields "works."

The direct techniques of social control are twofold. They include a simple set of rules which is communicated to every boy upon his admission and the prerogative of the director to return a boy to court for another disposition with the approval of the judge. The fact that some of the staff members attempt to discipline a boy by giving him "hours in the pit" for violating a rule pacifies the employee, but is not very effective in regulating the conduct of most boys. The knowledge, however, that the director can return a boy to court and occasionally does so, acts as a deterrant, especially for the adaptive, sophisticated, well organized delinquent. To these boys it means simply that commitment to the reformatory is a reality. In many respects, this fact acts as a sort of backstop and reinforces the other social controls.

A third intramural problem—one which was mentioned briefly in Chapter 3—involves a staff member who has a most difficult role to play, namely the sociological intern. He is a graduate student in the field of sociology who is employed for a period of one year. He receives training and experience in the techniques of guided group interaction and assists the director in the performance of various administrative duties. The major difficulty which all interns have stems from the fact that he is like a man without a country. The boys realize that he is a trainee and assume he is naïve in the ways of delinquents. Also, they learn soon after his arrival that, although he is an adult and an employee, he has little authority. The more sophisticated boys soon take advantage of this fluid situation by defining it in their own terms. One intern explained his experiences in this regard as follows: "The boys have taken advantage of me, disobeyed me, challenged me, questioned me, and have tried to make me one of the boys.

When I have taken boys to a candy store, they occasionally have devised ways for staying longer than they should. For example, one boy wrote letters while the other boys were buying sodas. When I said that it was time to leave, he insisted on making a phone call. At work, when I have substituted for the work supervisor, the boys ask me to give them laundry or some other jobs. On these occasions I explain that the jobs have already been assigned but some of them reply, 'Oh you can do it.' One time when I was conducting a group meeting two boys threatened me. One of them asked me why I didn't punish boys by giving them 'hours in the pit.' Another interrupted and said, 'You better not give hours. We're planning to initiate Pop and we'll initiate you too.' The boys questioned me about the limits of my authority by asking me if I can send boys home, send boys back to court, or if I can give furloughs. Also they want to know if I feel a boy is ready to go home and if I think he will stay out of trouble. Several boys have tried to make me one of the boys. One Saturday afternoon, a boy said to me 'You ought to hang with the boys more so they can get to know you. None of the boys know how to talk to you. They're afraid they will say the wrong thing.' Another boy told me 'That way you'll get hep, keep up to date, know what's going on in the world.' "

Each intern must find his own role and work out a definition of his status through his experiences with the boys. One of the factors that assists him greatly in this process is the group sessions. When he assumes direction of a therapy group under the supervision of the director the boys tend to see his role more clearly. He becomes in the eyes of the boys "a guy who is learning about us so he can work with boys in trouble, just like Mr. E—— (the director)." In time, the limits of his authority become more or less clearly established and thereby he gains acceptance by the boys as a person with status.

An additional set of problems arise as a consequence of crisis situations for individual boys and for a group of boys as well. These situations tend to develop around extreme forms of behavior which one or more boys engage in. The destruction of expensive property, the theft of a car, hostile, aggressive, clique behavior, and the return of a boy to court are all typical examples of actions that become crises for the boys. In fact, for some groups an act of little consequence can be exaggerated and develop into a near crisis.

Boys who run away can create crisis for the group also, especially if they commit another offense before they are caught. As a rule, when a boy runs away, the probation department is notified of his absence and the responsibility for apprehending him rests with it. Boys will try occasionally to deter someone who wants to run away, sometimes by physically sitting on him. Occasionally a runaway is returned to court for further action. It was necessary to make this decision in the case of a boy who kept running away every week for several weeks, each time taking with him an additional boy. Boys run away for a variety of reasons, although the motives are not always clearly understood, as in the case of the boy who left behind the following letter to the director:

Dear Mr. E——:

I am running away because I am sick of the boys saying that I'm a punk because I won't fight them, I cann't help myself no more. I'm afraid there'll be trouble if I do hang around. The boys don't understand me to well. I'm not happy that I'm running away. Please forgive me if you can for what I am about to do. I no it's not right what I'm going to do. I'm getting homesick for my mother. And I think that its best I say good-by to her before I go. I am going to see if I can get in the Navy if I can. Mr. E—— do you think I'm wrong about what I'm about to do? I hope you aren't because I have always been told I'm wrong about what I'm doing so that's why I going to run away from Highfields. I feel that I couldn't get along with the boys because I'm not the kind to look for fights and fool around. Everything I do the boys laugh at and make fun of me. Please try to understand me I don't thing its your fault that this has happened.

Joe   So Long

Another crisis situation develops out of the problem of homosexuality. There are occasions when one or more boys attempt to engage another boy in homosexual conduct. Also, it is possible for a homosexual to be selected for admission without prior knowledge by the court. Highfields is more fortunate than most institutions, and homosexuality is not a frequent problem. The pressures to engage in homosexual conduct which are present in most institutions are absent at Highfields. For example, exposure by the staff is a fairly simple matter. By observing sudden shifts in peer-group associations, a staff member can suspect or even detect this kind of behavior. Also, there is little prestige accorded boys who engage in homosexual relations because of the traditions that only boys who demonstrate that they have changed can go home. There are other factors at Highfields which minimize the sexual problems that develop in one-sex societies. The short period of residence coupled with the fact that contacts with the community are fairly frequent makes it possible for the boys to accommodate themselves to the absence of female companionship. Then, too, the attempt to exclude homosexuals from consideration for admission serves to minimize the importance of this problem at Highfields.

Although we have stated that the design of the program is neither fixed nor inviolate, it is important to caution that no single feature of the program can account for the success of the work at Highfields. The type of work situation which requires that the boys in residence leave the confines of the Highfields property is as important to the program as are the opportunities for contact with the community and the guided group interaction sessions. Each phase of the program is intimately related to every other phase to the extent that a change in one will result in a change in all. From time to time we have had to modify some of the features. Effects on all of the others soon became apparent, whether it involved cancelling the group meetings for two or three days, or assigning all the boys to work on the grounds for a period of time, as is done in the case of a snow storm or a hurricane. It would probably be futile to select one aspect of the program and superimpose it on an existing traditional framework. The unity of the program is not sacred, but it is crucial.

Appendix A

THE EXPRESSED NEED WHICH THE HIGHFIELDS PROPOSAL FULFILLED was first voiced by the courts in June, 1949. Some judges had expressed reluctance to send youthful offenders to reformatories for indeterminate sentences having relatively long maximums and average periods of residence of twelve to sixteen or eighteen months before parole. A Committee of County Judges on the Improvement of Sentencing and Probation Procedures, meeting with representatives of the Correction Division of the Department of Institutions and Agencies, recommended, among other things, changes in existing law to permit courts to impose short fixed-term reformatory sentences of from three to six months.

Department representatives saw objections to this plan, which were summarized in a letter addressed to the late Judge Joseph E. Conlon by Commissioner Sanford Bates under date of June 8, 1949. This letter said in part:

In the matter of the proposed short indeterminate sentence to the reformatories for men, with the judge establishing both a minimum and maximum, we have strong objection based on the fact that the presence in the reformatories of men with this type of sentence would complicate the matter of handling the majority of inmates serving institutional sentences. However, on the way back to Trenton on Saturday, Colonel Bixby expressed a view that such sentences as you propose might have great value in many cases, and he suggests the possibility of our opening up a small unit to handle only young men under this type of commitment. He suggests that such a unit might do an intensive job of correctional therapy under a plan whereby the court would place the offender on probation, specifying as a condition of such probation that the offender shall submit himself for a period of not less than three nor more than six months therapy in the special unit referred to above. Following such an in-

tensive course of treatment, the offender would return to probation.
It seems to me that this suggestion has many merits.

This concept had been developed somewhat more in detail in
an earlier memorandum from Deputy Commissioner Bixby to
Commissioner Bates dated June 6, 1949. The memorandum states:

The more I have thought about the suggestion for short-term treatment
facilities for delinquent boys which grew out of our conference with
Judge Conlon's committee on Saturday, the more I believe that it
presents an opportunity to undertake a very significant piece of pio-
neering and research. It is directly in line with what we had always
planned to do . . . at Chillicothe, but I think our present situation
enjoys two great advantages over that at the Reformatory: First, our
knowledge has increased to the point where we can construct a better
program, Second, I believe that we could set it up under less coercive
conditions which would give the boys we are working with better
motivations.

As I see it, the project would be set up along these lines:

A. The Lindbergh place would be set up to accommodate a limited
number of boys—not more than 25 at a time.

B. In selected cases of boys between the ages of 16 and 19, the courts
would put them on probation with the condition that they submit
themselves to a course of treatment at Highfields for a period of
not less than three nor more than six months.

C. At the conclusion of the period of treatment the boy would be
returned to the community to complete his probated sentence.

If we go through with this plan I think it is very important that we
do not just reproduce some of the old individualized treatment patterns which have never seemed to be applicable on anything like a
large scale. I think we should base the Highfields therapeutic program
on the group living basis and capitalize on the development of the
informal group relations of the boys with group psychotherapy playing a major role.

We could match the success or failure of the boys who go through
the project against:

A. Those who go on probation with this type of therapy, and

B. Selected matching cases of boys who go through the conventional
reformatory-parole sequence.

It seems to me that this proposed project has great possibilities and rather extensive implications if it succeeds. As I was thinking about it yesterday, I recall Doctor Loeser's very penetrating critique of the centralization of correctional measures for young persons when he was on the Board at the State Home for Girls.

I would rather expect that if our project succeeded to a substantial degree, the larger counties would want to establish their own intensive treatment centers and that we would find ourselves conducting High-fields only for the smaller counties which could not support such a project. Certainly if it kept a substantial number of boys out of State reformatories it would save a lot of money for all concerned; and it involves such a relatively small investment to try it out that I do not see how we can afford not to do it.

The Committee of County Judges was favorably inclined to the suggestion and felt that it might meet their needs.

Nothing further was done, however, until September of that year, when the late Mr. Sam Lewisohn made it known that the New York Foundation would be interested in giving financial support to a worthwhile experimental project in penology.

In response to this information, the following outline of a project was forwarded to the Foundation in support of a request for funds.

A PLAN FOR THE SHORT-TERM TREATMENT
OF YOUTHFUL OFFENDERS

Objectives of the plan:

Judges, when sentencing youthful offenders, usually have to choose between probation, an indeterminate sentence to a reformatory, or a short jail sentence. This is not always a satisfactory choice. Frequently the offender has been caught up in a whirlwind of car stealing, joy riding, girl chasing, and other forms of excitement and it is necessary to interrupt the rhythm of a social activities. He may be basically sound in his physical and mental make-up, but if he has not gained the social maturity consistent with his age he is not a suitable subject for probation at the time sentence is imposed.

On the other hand, an indeterminate sentence to a reformatory rarely results in parole in less than twelve months, and many experienced judges and penologists believe that a substantial number of youths can be started on the road to rehabilitation in a much shorter period.

Short jail sentences are generally acknowledged to be more harmful than beneficial because of the unfavorable associations and absence of constructive influences.

The plan proposed herein offers the court another alternative to which we have given the name "short-term treatment." The author's first-hand observation of many hundreds of young men committed to reformatories indicates that many of them can be ready for community supervision in from four to six months if new techniques of bringing about social maturation are applied in a concentrated way.

The plan is proposed as an experiment and demonstration to test the validity of a new approach to the treatment of selective young offenders. It is not intended to be applied to persons with serious constitutional inadequacies, deep-seated psychiatric difficulties, or delinquency patterns so persistent over a period of years as to suggest habitual criminality. It is intended for that group of young persons who seem to be not quite prepared psychologically for probation but who are possessed of the capacity to achieve readiness under the program outlined.

If the plan proves to be successful in a substantial number of cases, projects such as are described herein would be established by larger counties and municipalities as integral parts of their probation system. Thus, a greater number of young offenders would be treated by local agencies in their own communities, and the State would deal only with those requiring long-term incarceration and treatment. It is anticipated that the plan would substantially reduce the number of young offenders committed to State institutions.

Pilot project:

It is proposed to establish a group-centered project for not more than twenty-five boys between the ages of seventeen and nineteen years. Located in an abandoned farmhouse (or rural residence such as the former home of Colonel Charles A. Lindbergh, now owned by the State of New Jersey), the routines and patterns of the conventional reformatory will be replaced by an informal, non-institutional atmosphere.

Every activity will be carefully oriented to emphasize the interdependence of individuals and to point up the necessity for accepting mutual responsibility. Every device will be used to build up a valid self-confidence as the only possible basis for a sound confidence in other people. The advantages of fulfilling the obligations of a good citizen in a democratic society will be demonstrated by participation in the small, carefully structured democratic society of the project itself. Real life situations which develop in the unit will provide opportunities to develop insight in the boys.

The success of the project will depend upon the careful selection of the director or leader who will be responsible for establishing and maintaining a therapeutic climate.

Since the core of the program will be guided group interaction, he must be skilled in that technique; and while professional training, intelligence and sound experience will be required, they must be combined with stability, inner security, and a warm feeling for and deep faith in mankind.

Other personnel will include a man and wife to supervise housekeeping activities and to assume the role of house-parents, and a "handyman" or "Jack-of-all-trades." It is important to note that no custodial personnel will be employed and no custodial responsibility will be exercised by the project since the residents will not be prisoners but boys on probation.

Admission to the Project:

Admissions will be, in a sense, voluntary. When a court is confronted with a youth deemed suitable for short-term treatment, the execution of sentence will be suspended on condition that he submit to treatment at the project for a period of not less than one nor more than six months. When the director notifies the court that treatment has achieved its maximum value the youth will be placed on regular probation in the community. It is estimated that the average young man will be returned to regular probation within four to six months and avoid the stigma of a reformatory commitment.

Outline of program:

The short-term treatment program will embrace a number of interrelated and carefully coordinated activities. Among them are:

(a) *Group interaction sessions.* Since the very essence of the program is to provide for constructive group experiences, all members of the community will attend guided group interaction sessions every day. These sessions provide experiences, somewhat akin to the well integrated family, which have previously been denied to the residents of the project. In the group meetings emphasis will be placed first of all upon the development of better insight on the past of the individual and of his own inadequacies. Basic principals of personality development, mental hygiene, and social relationships will be taught by the application of group therapy methods instead of through conventional didactic techniques. The boys will be assisted, in the group sessions, to foresee and prepare for the problems and pitfalls, as well as the obligations and opportunities, they will face upon their return to the community. It is this direct attack against the problem which differentiates the present proposal from other systems of institutional treatment.

(b) *Individual counselling.* The small number of boys in the project at any one time will enable the director to devote more attention to intensive individual counselling for boys who need it to achieve more effective group participation.

(c) *Self-government.* The group will evolve its own rules and regulations and, under the guidance of the director, be responsible for enforcing them. Because the project does not exercise custodial responsibility, self-government will be possible at a level which has never been practical in a typical correctional or penal institution. Rules and regulations need only to embrace common sense restrictions which people have to observe in order to live together; and the severest punishment meted out to a non-conformist will be expulsion from the group. This so far from the situation in conventional correctional institutions, where non-conformity brings a prolonged period of residence and a denial of opportunities for adjustment, that it constitutes one of the major advantages of the proposed plan.

(d) *Individual project.* It is considered highly desirable that every individual select and complete a project during his period in the unit. It might be writing a short story, building a radio cabinet, overhauling a gasoline engine, or almost anything else that the individual feels he would like to do.

(e) *Other activities.* The daily life of the residents will be rounded out by other activities, including work, religious training, recreation, and socially directed educational acitivities.

The work will be "real" work as opposed to "made" work. Among other things, the maintenance of the unit, reforestation and soil conservation, truck gardening, and assisting in the care of institutionally confined patients have the kind of social significance which is desirable for a project of this kind. No attempt will be made to give vocational training.

In the educational field, no organized or standardized school is contemplated but individualized academic training for those who feel a real need in specialized areas will be available. For the most part, educational efforts will take the form of discussion groups centering around newspapers, radio programs and current periodicals which will give the residents an opportunity to evaluate and interpret the information and opinions with which these media constantly bombard the individual in our complex social structure.

It is hoped that religious training and experience will be available in nearby community churches.

Research:

Much of the value of the pilot project described in this paper will be lost if a careful scientific evaluation of its results is not provided. It is hoped that funds will be made available to establish an independent research study under a committee of qualified specialists in social and related sciences. The members of this committee should not be associated with the project in any administrative capacity and should conduct their study from a completely independent point of view.

As may be seen from the foregoing formulation, an independent evaluation of the plan's effectiveness was considered to avoid the danger of producing merely another "fad." Mr. Barklie Henry of Princeton, then a member of the Board of Managers of the New Jersey Diagnostic Center, had followed the development of the Highfields idea from its inception. He was intensely interested in the idea and made many helpful suggestions regarding it; through his efforts the Vincent Astor Foundation became interested in supporting a research study.

Copies of the statement of the "Plan for the Short-Term Treatment of Youthful Offenders" were furnished to the trustees of the Astor Foundation and a meeting was held on January 18, 1950, in Trenton. Present were Mrs. Vincent Astor, Mr. William Jackson, and Mr. Barklie Henry of the Astor Foundation, Commissioner Bates, Dr. Bixby, and Mr. McCorkle.

While the two foundations were considering the advisability of making grants for the proposed venture, the State proceeded to put the property in shape to receive boys by July 1, 1950.

Appendix B

Signed by Governor Robert B. Meyner 21 June 1957
Now *CHAPTER 90, P.L. 1957*

SENATE, No. 173

STATE OF NEW JERSEY

Introduced March 18, 1957
By Senator Shershin

Referred to Committee on Institutions, Public Health and Welfare

An Act authorizing the Department of Institutions and Agencies to establish facilities throughout the State for receiving and treating juvenile delinquent probationers on a short term voluntary basis, providing a method for defraying the cost thereof and supplementing Title 30 of the Revised Statutes.

WHEREAS, The experimental facility heretofore established by the Department of Institutions and Agencies at the site of the former Lindbergh Estate, and known as "Highfields," has proven to be a highly desirable and successful method of providing treatment and therapy for juvenile probationers, on a short-term basis, where the juvenile court has directed the juvenile offender to accept voluntary residential treatment at such facility as a condition of probation; and

WHEREAS, Such facilities have been recognized as providing an effective method for dealing with juvenile offenders on a preventive treatment basis prior to institutional commitment by actual experience in New Jersey for the past 6 years at "Highfields"; and

WHEREAS, IT appears desirable and necessary to expand this program by the establishment of additional such facilities in various parts of the State; now, therefore

BE IT ENACTED by the Senate and General Assembly of the State of New Jersey:

1. It is hereby declared to be the public policy of this State to adopt

and use every practical program, technique and procedure in order to establish in New Jersey the most effective methods for the prevention and treatment of juvenile delinquency without institutional confinement under court commitment procedures wherever possible.

2. The Department of Institutions and Agencies therefore is authorized to establish, equip and maintain facilities in various parts of the State for receiving and treating juvenile delinquent probationers under circumstances where a juvenile court has directed, as a condition of probation of such offender that he voluntarily submit to treatment and supervision, for a period not to exceed 4 months, in a facility under direction, control and supervision of said department.

3. The department shall establish such facilities in such areas of the State as are best calculated to carry out the purposes of this act and shall maintain therein preventive treatment programs, guided group interaction, and such other procedures as are deemed most adequate to deal with youthful offenders in an effort to prevent further delinquency.

4. Except as otherwise provided for herein, the management, operation and administration of such facilities shall be in conformity with the provisions of Title 30, Revised Statutes, and the State Board of Control of Institutions and Agencies shall promulgate such reasonable rules and regulations as shall be necessary to effectuate the purposes of this act.

5. The management, direction and control of such facilities shall be vested in the Commissioner of the Department of Institutions and Agencies. No board of managers shall be appointed and the commissioner shall perform those duties and functions which would otherwise be performed by such board.

6. There is hereby appropriated from the general funds of the State Treasury, the sum of $150,000.00 to the Department of Institutions and Agencies for the purpose of carrying out the provisions of this act.